WHEN DOVES TRY

ISRAEL'S PEACE NOW MOVEMENT 1978-1983 —

WITH AN EPILOGUE FOR
THE POST-OCTOBER 7 WORLD

MICAH L. SIFRY

NONE OF THE ABOVE ENTERPRISES

Cover photo: "The Peace Now (Shalom Achshav) movement organized a march protesting against the government policy at the Poleg junction." Dan Hadani collection / National Library of Israel / The Pritzker Family National Photography Collection / CC BY 4.0

Library of Congress Control Number: 2025921424

ISBN: 979-8-9932636-1-8

For the next generation

"*To do your first works over means to reexamine everything. Go back to where you started, or as far back as you can, examine all of it, travel your road again and tell the truth about it. Sing or shout or testify or keep it to yourself: but know whence you came.*"

—James Baldwin

"*These are the times that try men's souls: The summer soldier and the sunshine patriot will, in this crisis, shrink from the service of his country; but he that stands it now, deserves the love and thanks of man and woman.*"

—Thomas Paine

CONTENTS

PROLOGUE

I FIRST VISITED Israel when I was five years old, in 1967. We traveled from New York, me, my mother and my younger sister, to spend the summer in the coastal city of Netanya with my aunt and uncle and their families. My father joined us midway through after he finished teaching summer school. I remember going to the beach, picnicking in pine woods with my Israeli cousins, and going on a two-day car trip to the south with my father and my uncle, who wanted to see the results of the Six-Day War first-hand. We may have gone into the Sinai, newly conquered by Israel, but I'm not sure. All I really recall is how hot it was to sit in the backseat with no air conditioning, staring out at dusty landscapes and making occasional stops to look at burnt-out tanks and half-tracks, debris from the just-finished war. I think we also took a trip to the Golan Heights, though I may be conflating that memory with another summer-long visit we made a few years later. We also visited Jerusalem, newly conquered with its ancient walled city "reunited" with the Jewish section to its west. If we went further into the West Bank, I can't recall.

I was too young to understand what I was seeing. But what to do with the lands Israel conquered in 1967—the Sinai, Gaza, the Golan Heights, the West Bank and East Jerusalem—is the question that has vexed the Middle East ever since that summer.

It wasn't until I was in my early teens that I first started to ask questions of my Israeli cousins. In 1975, when I was thirteen and we visited for another summer, I remember wondering why the license plates on cars in Israel had two different colors and Hebrew letters alongside the numbers on some of them. One older cousin told me, "That's how we know which cars belong to Arabs." The letters corresponded to the name of the city they were from, she added. I said something like, we would never make Black people in America drive cars with different color license plates. She said, it's different here. We need to keep an eye on them. Even though I was just a kid, the casual racism expressed by my cousins bothered me.

In the early 1970s, back home in New York, I got involved with Hashomer Hatzair, a Socialist-Zionist youth movement that my father had also belonged to decades earlier. I started to learn more about the socialist values of many of Israel's founders, and at the movement's sleep-away camp in the Catskills I made lifelong friends, met my future wife, and dreamt of utopia living on kibbutz. Those were turbulent times to come of age as an American Jew. Israel's victory in the 1967 Six-Day War had awakened a newly assertive pride in one's Jewishness, while the Yom Kippur War of 1973 reminded everyone that Israel was not invincible. At that time, a lot of the American Jewish community's new-found energy flowed into advocacy for oppressed Soviet Jewry. But inside the youth movement, our leaders were already focusing on a more central fight—the future of the occupied territories—echoing what their older peers living in Israel were also doing.

So, my first exposure to Peace Now (Shalom Ackshav) came from inside the same political movement that helped support its emergence in Israel. I don't know when I first heard of the organization, but I do remember marching with other kids from Hashomer Hatzair in the Israel Day Parade down Manhattan's Fifth Ave in May 1978, wearing our blue *chultzot* with white strings in the lapel—the uniform of our youth movement—and holding signs supporting Peace Now. Along the march route, some watchers heckled us and called us "traitors." Afterwards, there was a festival in Central Park for all the participants where we had a booth with Peace Now banners and leaflets. People from the Jewish Defense League and Betar, the far-right youth movement aligned with Menachem Begin, who was then Israel's prime minister, came over to harass us.

When I got to college, my connection to Israel deepened. I spent the second semester of my freshman year living on Kibbutz Shomrat with other friends from my Hashomer Hatzair cohort. My fluency in Hebrew, which was already passable from years of family visits, got better. And upon returning back to the US, my commitment to the youth movement intensified further, as several dozen of us formed a *garin* (Hebrew for seed) and prepared to make Aliyah together to live on Kibbutz Adamit, on Israel's border with Lebanon.

That's how I came to spend the summer of 1982, between my junior and senior years at Princeton University, living on Adamit and traveling around the country talking to leaders and activists in Israel's peace movement. It was a perfect confluence of personal and intellectual interests for me. The kibbutz welcomed those of us who were planning to eventually make Aliyah there, expecting that a summer visit would serve to strengthen our commitment to make such a life-changing decision.

My then-girlfriend (and eventual wife) and I arrived at Adamit around June 9th, fresh off attending a giant rally in New York's Central Park the prior weekend that was organized by the US nuclear freeze movement. Israel's 1982 invasion of Lebanon had started a few days earlier, on June 6th. Our friends who had arrived at the kibbutz earlier that June told us of watching long convoys of military equipment rolling past in the first days; they knew from what they saw that this was probably not the "limited" incursion Israel's leaders were claiming it would be. Indeed, even though we could see the border fence from the kibbutz dining room, the war was much further to the north. Other than the fighter jets that would sometimes streak past, it was not at our doorstep. We slept in housing for volunteers, not in shelters. And starting with the second Saturday after the war began, we traveled in the kibbutz's vans to join the growing demonstrations against the war that were called first by new groups like Yesh Gvul (There is a Limit) and then embraced and amplified by Peace Now.

That summer I spent half my time working in Adamit's corn fields and avocado groves, and the other half in Tel Aviv and Jerusalem, interviewing peace activists and political journalists who covered the movement. I also spent a few days digging through *The Jerusalem Post*'s extensive archive of English news clippings, which I supplemented with other forays into the Hebrew press. I attended two meetings of Peace Now's central committee, listening as they debated how to respond to the war. And I also sat in on one of the first organizing meetings of Yesh Gvul in Jerusalem, listening as thirty-or-so activists crammed into someone's living room debated the merits of refusing to serve in the war versus serving and then having greater standing to protest.

I was having the same debate with myself. I knew that if we were to uproot ourselves and come live in Israel, I would have to serve in the army —an obligation that every able-bodied non-ultra-religious Israeli Jew accepts upon turning eighteen. As a slightly older immigrant, I would have a somewhat shortened period of service, but I'd still be required to do reserve duty every year until middle age. As someone with very strong pacifist leanings, I wasn't sure this was a commitment I wanted to make. But at the same time, everyone told us that if you wanted to be able to fully participate in Israeli public life, failing to do one's army service would be unacceptable.

We returned to the United States in late August in time for the start of my senior year at Princeton. Around that same time, the Palestine Liberation Organization left besieged Beirut under the terms of the cease-fire that ended the war. Two weeks later, the massacre of thousands of Palestinian civilians in the Sabra and Shatila refugee camps of Beirut took place. It was committed by rightwing Christian militias who were allies of Israel's government and under the watchful eyes of the Israeli army. A week after that, answering the call of Peace Now and the opposition Labor Party, more than 400,000 Israelis—ten percent of what was then the country's population—rallied in Tel Aviv to protest and demand a full investigation of Israel's responsibility for the crime. A government commission eventually concluded that the IDF bore indirect responsibility for enabling the massacre, forcing Defense Minister Ariel Sharon—the architect of Israel's invasion and Peace Now's arch-enemy—to resign.

It was with all these events and experiences as backdrop that I sat down to write a study of Peace Now's early years. What follows is not the whole story of the movement, but rather mainly a chronicle of its rise in the late 1970s and early 1980s in response to Egyptian President Anwar Sadat's peace overture to Israel, its role in pressuring Prime Minister Begin to go to Camp David and come to a peace deal, and its subsequent struggle to challenge Israel's increasingly powerful settlement movement. The latter was determined to maintain Israel's grip on the occupied territories and, with

20-20 hindsight, clearly had the upper hand throughout the years that followed.

I submitted my senior thesis to the Princeton Politics Department in the spring of 1983, with the title "Shalom Ackshav: The Rise and Role of Israel's Peace Movement." To my surprise and delight, the department gave it the prize for best senior thesis that year. After I graduated, one of my academic mentors, the former New York Times war correspondent Gloria Emerson, who taught a highly-sought-after class in journalism, sent a copy to her friend Victor Navasky, the editor of *The Nation* magazine, with the suggestion that he consider publishing an excerpt. He invited me in for coffee. And after a friendly (but to me very intimidating) meeting in his office, he urged me to apply for an internship. I was accepted and started learning the craft of journalism in a serious way that fall, making the humble sum of $50 a week.

Though *The Nation* didn't publish anything from my thesis—probably because it had already covered Peace Now—the internship did offer me a chance to write for the magazine. My first published piece there was a short editorial about Israel's triple-digit hyper-inflation crisis, and how its right-wing government was trying to hold onto power by printing too many shekels and handing out subsidies to its political base. If memory serves, the editorial also chastised the Reagan Administration for continuing to give Israel billions in economic and military aid, propping it up. I also started freelancing for other publications, like *The Progressive*, which published an article in 1984 on the challenges facing the peace movement after the Lebanon War.[1] Later, I got to write more about the Israel-Palestine issue, including an in-depth report for *The Nation* on the first intifada, which broke out in December 1987 while I was there for a visit.

Over the years I worked for *The Nation*, through 1996, I also wrote many of the magazine's unsigned editorials about the conflict. It was a challenge. The magazine was historically very supportive of the Jewish state; in the 1940s its then-editor Freda Kirchwey was a vocal supporter of Zionism. So was contributing editor I. F. Stone, though in his later years he became quite critical of Israel's treatment of the Palestinians. The magazine

---

1. Micah L. Sifry, "Israel at War with Itself: Lebanon puts loyalties to the test," *The Progressive*, August 1984.

was still in the thick of those conflicts in the 1980s and 1990s, but I'm proud to say it was an early supporter of recognizing the Palestine Liberation Organization as the legitimate representative of the Palestinian people, and it endorsed Rev. Jesse Jackson for the Democratic presidential nomination in 1988, in part because of his principled advocacy for the Palestinian right to self-determination alongside Israel. Columbia professor Edward Said, perhaps the most famous and influential Palestinian-American intellectual and advocate of his time, wrote often for the magazine, and he once told me how much he appreciated my contributions to the magazine's editorial stance on the conflict.

Getting that internship at *The Nation* in 1983 altered the course of my life. The opportunity to get in on the ground floor of one of America's oldest and more influential opinion magazines was too good to pass up. My wife and I changed our plans and told our friends, some of whom were already living on Kibbutz Adamit, and others that were packing their belongings to go, that we wouldn't be joining them. At the time it was a very hard decision to make. But eventually, we came to believe it was the right one for us. It certainly resolved my dilemma about needing to do military service if I wanted to participate in Israeli society.

As I got further into my career as a journalist, I started to branch away from writing about Israel-Palestine. After reporting on the first intifada in early 1988, I wrote a long essay for *Middle East Report* (MERIP) about how the issue was roiling the Democratic party, called "Jesse and the Jews: Palestine and the Struggle for the Democratic Party."[2] A few years later, I wrote a cover essay for *The Nation* titled "Antisemitism in the Mind of America."[3]

Everything I covered in those pieces is still relevant today. Progressives are still fighting inside the Democratic party to shift US foreign policy away from unconditional support for Israel. The so-called pro-Israel American Jewish establishment is still weaponizing the charge of antisemitism to favor its political allies on the right (because they are such knee-jerk supporters of Israel) and attack its political critics on the left (because they talk about Palestinian rights). Starting in the early 1990s, I began to feel

---

2. *Middle East Report*, November/December 1988.
3. *The Nation*, January 25, 1993.

that there wasn't anything new or valuable I could add to this discourse. Plus, the idea of devoting my career solely to the fraught politics of Israel-Palestine, where everyone seems to watch everyone else's words with a laser-beam and argue endlessly over every dispute, felt depressing.

COMING BACK TO ISRAEL-PALESTINE

So, for much of my career I've focused my attention on American politics, with an emphasis on democracy, organizing, independent political movements and technology. Those remain my primary interests. Why then am I choosing now to publish a book about Peace Now?

I have three reasons. First, in recent years, I decided to re-engage in the Israel-Palestine issue as part of my work as an organizer. After suffering for many years with rightwing Democratic hawk Eliot Engel as my congressman, I saw an opportunity to assist Jamaal Bowman, a progressive educator who challenged and defeated Engel in the 2020 Democratic primary. Bowman ran for office with a clear commitment to elevating Palestinian rights alongside Israel, and I wanted to try to help him navigate the challenges that would come his way representing one of the most Jewish House districts in America. So, as a volunteer, I got involved with Jews for Racial and Economic Justice, a New York City-based group that had a sister PAC, The Jewish Vote, which endorsed Bowman early on. I also joined the local Westchester chapter of J Street, the "pro-Israel, pro-peace, pro-democracy" lobby that is the liberal Zionist counterweight to AIPAC.[4]

---

4. My work with Bowman was only partially successful, and less so as time went on and he decided to adopt an increasingly shrill anti-Zionist position while representing one of the most Jewish districts in the country. In 2022, he held off two primary challengers, but in 2024 he was defeated by the Democratic Westchester county executive, George Latimer—who was backed by an unprecedented $20 million in outside spending by AIPAC and other groups. For more, see my Substack posts: *"Jamaal Bowman, George Latimer and The Israel-Gaza War at Home"* from May 24, 2024 (https://theconnector.substack.com/p/jamaal-bowman-george-latimer-and); *"All Politics is Local: Notes on NY CD-16 as Primary Day Approaches"* from June 6, 2024 (https://theconnector.substack.com/p/all-politics-is-local-notes-on-ny); then scroll to the middle of *"On Antisemitism and the Fight for Democracy,"* from June 12, 2024 (https://theconnector.substack.com/p/on-antisemitism-and-the-fight-for); then read *"The Empire Strikes Back: Latimer v Bowman Goes Down to the Wire"* from June 21, 2024 (https://theconnector.substack.com/p/the-empire-strikes-back-latimer-v), and finally *"The Road Not Taken: Hard Truths about*

When Israel's pro-democracy protest movement took to the streets in January of 2023, building on more than a decade of growing opposition to the dominance of Prime Minister Bibi Netanyahu and his alliance with the religious right, and successfully holding the line against his worst initiatives with weekly demonstrations that often drew tens of thousands of participants, I found myself drawn to re-engaging further. That's because there were lessons that the Israeli movement could teach American pro-democracy organizers about how to push back against authoritarianism, and I wrote a long, reported essay about that for *The New Republic* in the summer of 2023.[5] Throughout my career I've been interested in how organizers build and sustain movements, so uplifting this early history of Peace Now and exploring how an all-volunteer-led movement could catch fire and then struggle to sustain itself is as relevant now as it was decades ago.

Then Hamas attacked Israel on October 7, 2023, massacring 1200 Israeli Jews, Arabs and foreigners, and traumatizing the entire country. In response, the leaders of the most rightwing government in Israel's history announced that there were no innocent Palestinians in Gaza and that they were subjecting the enclave to a total siege. Here in America, the liberal-left coalition shattered, as people who previously thought they were allies picked sides. Either you were pro-Israel, or you were pro-Hamas, some decided. Conversely, if you weren't pro-Palestine, you were pro-genocide, the other side said.

In my weekly Substack newsletter *The Connector*,[6] I found myself drawing on all my experience writing editorials decades earlier for The Nation, arguing against this either/or binary and for the only understanding of the conflict that makes any sense: that seven million Israeli Jews and seven million Palestinian Arabs live between the Jordan River and the Mediterranean Sea, and *none of them are going anywhere*. That core truth is what animated Peace Now from day one and still animates the much smaller peace forces in Israel-Palestine today. It would do a world of good if today's generation of pro-Palestinian activists recognized that

---

Jamaal Bowman's Loss," from July 1, 2024 (https://theconnector.substack.com/p/the-empire-strikes-back-latimer-v).

5. "What Can Americans Learn from the Israeli Protests? A Lot," *The New Republic*, July 13, 2023.

6. See TheConnector.substack.com.

instead of rejecting all Israelis as equally evil, strengthening the moderate, anti-occupation/pro-peace side of Israel would fundamentally help Palestinians too.

With that understanding top of mind, I decided to travel to Israel-Palestine in March of 2024 on a study and solidarity tour organized by Americans for Peace Now (which has since merged with another group and goes by the name New Jewish Narrative). Though I had been back many times since the 1980s, I wanted to see for myself how the country had changed and what it was going through because of this new chapter of the conflict. I also wanted to reconnect with family and friends who live there, since, despite everything, life must go on and the bonds of friendship and fraternity run deeper than disagreements over politics. I particularly was attracted to traveling with Americans for Peace Now because it is Shalom Ackshav's sister organization in the United States. I knew we would have a chance to spend time with current and past leaders of Peace Now while we were visiting. This book includes a long epilogue that I've written to share my impressions of that time together and to report on the state of Israel's peace movement today. Think of it as a bookend to a forty-year story.

Finally, in publishing this book, I want to add my small contribution to the unfinished work of documenting and advancing peace and social justice activism in Israel-Palestine. Even though the rapprochement between Israel and the PLO in the 1990s ultimately failed, thanks to the most successful political assassination in modern history (the killing by a rightwing activist of Prime Minister Yitzhak Rabin as he left a peace rally in Tel Aviv in 1995), ongoing settlement expansion, and a deliberate campaign of suicide bombings against Israeli civilians carried out by Hamas and, to a lesser extent, the Palestinian Authority, in the late 1990s and early 2000s, the peace movement in Israel-Palestine has never died.

Peace Now itself has evolved from leading mass demonstrations into the leading research organization tracking the never-ending efforts of the Jewish settlement movement. Amazingly, Hagit Ofran, the longtime leader of Peace Now's widely respected Settlement Watch program, is the granddaughter of Yeshayahu Leibowitz, an iconoclastic academic who was one of the first and most vociferous opponents of the occupation and settlement of the West Bank. Other groups now lead the demonstrations against

Israel's rightwing government, which I touch on in the book's epilogue. But there is a long and unbroken thread of work that connects all of this, from the earliest advocacy of cultural Zionists like Ahad Ha'am, Judas Magnes and Martin Buber for a binational homeland for Jews and Palestinians, to the precursors of Peace Now in groups like the Movement for Peace and Security, to the more recent efforts like Breaking the Silence and B'Tselem to oppose the occupation and defend Palestinian rights.

WHAT PEACE NOW'S RISE STILL TEACHES US

The early years of Peace Now show that brave people can change the course of history. Egyptian President Anwar Sadat took a risk by traveling to Israel in November 1977, breaking the taboo in the Arab world against direct contact with the Jewish state. He offered Israel a genuine and lasting peace but, in exchange, asked for it to withdraw from all the territories it had conquered in 1967. Israeli Prime Minister Menachem Begin balked, torn between his hopes and his fears, and beholden to a vision that saw those conquered lands not as bargaining chips but as *Eretz Israel Hashlema* —Greater Israel, the Jewish people's biblical patrimony. In that pregnant moment, the emergence of the Peace Now movement, and its ability to galvanize hundreds of thousands of Israelis, was crucial to forcing Begin's hand. It led to the first crucial step towards ending the age-old conflict: peace between Israel and its largest Arab neighbor.

Today we are at a similar crossroads, though the path forward is far less clear. The war between Israel and Hamas in Gaza has seemed intractable. Both sides believe that they can win—Israel by crushing Hamas, and Hamas first by expanding the conflict to the West Bank, Lebanon and ultimately the entire region, and now by forcing Israel to accept a stalemate along with the release of hundreds or thousands of imprisoned Palestinians in exchange for the Israeli hostages it has held since October 7. Israeli Prime Minister Netanyahu has also feared for his own political future in the event of an end to the hostilities, because he is on trial for corruption. As long as the war continues, he can delay that accounting and maintain his governing coalition. And in both Israeli and Palestinian societies, each side believes the other is committed to their annihilation. It has been a fight to the death.

And yet, an alternative path beckons. It is not just the one that U.S. President Joe Biden tried to offer: A potential alliance of moderate Sunni nations is willing to normalize relations with Israel if it exits Gaza and commits to a future Palestinian state. It is the potential of mutual coexistence. A joint poll conducted over the summer of 2024 by the Palestinian Center for Policy and Survey Research (PSR) in Ramallah and the International Program in Conflict Resolution and Mediation at Tel Aviv University found plenty of evidence that Israelis and Palestinians believe the worst of the other side.[7] But the study also found a silver lining: that if each side took brave steps meant to break the cycle of violence and oppression, popular opinion would shift and a majority would support a comprehensive peace deal.

Those brave steps would not be easy—the Israeli government would have to agree to acknowledge Palestinians' historic link to the land, offer to pay compensation to Palestinian refugees for the loss of their homes and land, and a commit to eventually release all the Palestinian prisoners it holds. On the other side, the Palestinian government would need to combat incitement against Israel and change its school textbooks to show that it was doing so, allow Israeli factories to keep operating in its territory, pay compensation to Jews who had to leave Arab countries after 1948, and commit to consolidate all armed factions into a single security force while disarming any others.

According to the poll, the prospect of those kinds of confidence-building moves shifted how both Israelis and Palestinians thought about compromise. When paired together as joint moves that would be taken in concert by both sides, the effect on public opinion was even stronger. It produced majority support among both communities for the following peace deal:

- a de-militarized Palestinian state,
- an Israeli withdrawal to the pre-1967 Green Line with equal territorial exchange,
- family unification in Israel for 100,000 Palestinian refugees,

---

7. Palestinian-Israeli Pulse: A Joint Poll, September 12, 2024, https://www.pcpsr.org/sites/default/files/Summary%20Report_%20English_Joint%20Poll%2012%20Sept%202024.pdf.

- West Jerusalem as the capital of Israel and East Jerusalem as the capital of Palestine,
- the Jewish Quarter and the Western Wall under Israeli sovereignty and the Muslim and Christian quarters and the al Haram al Sharif/Temple Mount under Palestinian sovereignty,
- Israel and the future state of Palestine will be democratic,
- the bilateral agreement will be part of a larger peace agreement with all Arab states,
- the US and major Arab countries will ensure full implementation of the agreement by both sides,
- and the end of the conflict and claims.

This suggests that the future is still fluid. Brave leaders and new political movements could shift the direction of the conflict from mutual annihilation to mutual coexistence. And that is why the history of what Peace Now helped do in its earliest years remains relevant today.

THE STORY AHEAD

Anwar Sadat's visit to Jerusalem in November of 1977 irrevocably shattered worldviews. For the first time an Arab leader had accepted Israel and offered it peace in return for territories captured in the 1967 war. The realization of Israel's yearning for peace, long expressed in song and prose, suddenly seemed possible. It was out of this combination of hope, frustration, and despair that the Peace Now movement was born and gained its footing.

I am fascinated by the rise of the Peace Now movement for many reasons. For one, it is an excellent source of insight into the genesis, expansion, problems, and potential of peace movements in general. But more importantly, it remains relevant today because of what it suggests about the path to the achievement of a comprehensive peace, including the acceptance of a historic compromise between the Israelis and the Palestinians. Forty-some years ago, a sizable number of Israeli Jews sought to shift their country towards a process of national self-searching and a rejection of paranoia, cynicism, chauvinism and the unrestrained use of force to "create facts" and "solve" political problems. As we all know, they were only partially successful. But something similar must again arise within Israel if the fourteen million humans living on the land between the river and the sea are ever to find some semblance of peace.

Though the movement itself arose, in part, as a reaction to the election of Israel's first rightwing prime minister, Menachem Begin, and in rejection of his explicit assertion of Israel's historic right to Greater Israel (i.e. including the West Bank and the Gaza Strip), its philosophical roots go back to the beginnings of Zionism. In general, mainstream Zionism either did not recognize the existence of the Arabs living in Palestine, dismissed the idea that there was a conflict of nationalisms brewing, or else recognized this fact and coldly advocated the gradual dispossession and dispersion of the Palestinian Arabs and the creation of Zionist "facts."

But at least a few Zionist leaders, men like Ahad Ha'am, Judah Magnes and Martin Buber, saw that the solution of the "Jewish question" created a genuine "Palestinian question," and therefore advocated various forms of compromise between the two peoples. This counter-tradition remained marginal during the early years of Israeli statehood, as the dominant Labor Party consolidated its Zionist vision—complete with the confiscation of Palestinian lands and systematic discrimination against Palestinian individuals and villages.

After the 1967 war, the dovish Movement for Peace and Security and other peace groups tried to fight the steps toward annexation that the Land of Israel Movement and the nationalist right sought. But they lacked public support—partially because they were seen as outside the realm of Zionist politics and partially because their option of trading territories for peace lacked a complementary response from the Arab world. And so the Labor Party slowly drifted towards the right, starting the process of annexation with East Jerusalem, settlements, and the economic integration of the occupied territories. Begin's Likud Party and its extra-parliamentary ally, the Gush Emunim ("Bloc of the Faithful") settlement movement, only sped this process with greater ideological fervor and state support.

Thus, Peace Now's opposition merely followed a long line of Israeli dissent. But what made the movement special, and worthy of study, is that, buoyed by Sadat's peace initiative, it successfully mobilized a significant segment of Israeli society around more than just the principle of exchanging territories for peace. Gradually, through its actions and statements, it advanced the simple notion that the Palestinian people exist, and some compromise must be reached between them and the Israeli people.

Peace Now was founded by reserve officers who explicitly positioned themselves within the Israeli national consensus and who argued in both moral and pragmatic terms for Israel's interests in not annexing the occupied territories. It began with a small group of reserve soldiers writing an open letter to the government demanding that it take a different path, which then struck a chord and mushroomed into a movement–a pattern that has occurred again and again in Israeli society. (Indeed it repeated again in the spring and summer of 2025, with thousands of reservists publicly declaring their opposition to continuing to serve in Netanyahu's war on Gaza.)

From the start the movement's leaders decided that it would be tactically wiser to unite a large segment of the public around broad principles of opposition to Begin's plans rather than fragment the movement over specific questions clarifying its stand on the eventual compromise for peace. They sought to be a big tent for a loyal opposition to war and occupation, rather than a political party with precise positions on a range of issues. This studied vagueness had the effect of making Begin's interpretation of Zionism look extreme and Peace Now's moderate. It helped save the movement from the fate of other peace groups that had explicitly advocated from their beginnings solutions like a Palestinian state. The movement's leaders were deliberately seeking not just to be politically correct, but to also be effective—to gradually transform Israeli attitudes on the core issue of Palestinian national rights and thereby save Israel from becoming another South Africa.

For both reasons of conviction and strategy, Peace Now avoided advocating radical tactics like the refusal of military service that they believed would completely alienate the Israeli public. At the time, this strategy paid off, for the movement was able to mobilize hundreds of thousands of Israelis around principles that gradually became more explicitly cognizant of Palestinian nationalism while being couched in terms of a Zionist analysis committed to the strengthening of Israel's security and progressive character.

The chapters of this book start with Peace Now's beginnings and rise preceding Camp David in 1978 and cover its long struggle over the future of the West Bank, its near disintegration prior to the 1981 elections, its rebirth as the situation on the West Bank deteriorated badly in the spring of 1982, and the cataclysm of the war in Lebanon and its aftermath.

Interwoven in this narrative are descriptions of the international and domestic developments that Peace Now was responding to. The salient issues, from the movement's point of view, were the danger that Begin's intransigence would torpedo the chances for peace with Egypt; the hastening annexation of the West Bank intended by the Begin government's settlement policy; the demagoguery, extremism and polarization marking the political climate; and the imperial war in Lebanon against Palestinian nationalism. As a movement that primarily reacted to events, Peace Now must be described in its context. The bulk of my sources were taped interviews with Peace Now leaders done between the summer of 1982 and the winter of 1983 and newspaper articles from the Israeli press.

The book finishes with an epilogue describing the cataclysmic effects of the October 7, 2023 Hamas attack and the efforts of Israeli-Palestinian peace groups to advance the cause of co-existence against the backdrop of a much intensified Israel versus Palestine binary.

MY BIASES AND ASSUMPTIONS

Implicit in the pages to follow are several underlying biases and assumptions that are important to make explicit from the start. In too much writing on the Arab-Israeli conflict claims to objectivity are advanced and hidden agendas denied. First, then, I should say that I remain committed to the concept of Zionism as a movement of Jewish national self-determination. I deplore, however, the racist and militarist forms it has taken from early on. Zionism today, if it is to achieve its goal of the normalization of the Jewish condition, must struggle for peace with the Arabs, a historic compromise with the Palestinians, and a just society with equality of rights for all the people living in Israel. Self-determination cannot include the oppression of another people. I recognize that this may be impossible, that Zionism itself stands in the way of such an outcome—in which case, as Shaul Magid argues in his 2023 book, *The Necessity of Exile*, Zionism has become a spent force, out of date and out of touch with the realities of

15

today.[8]

The problem is that unquestioning support for Israel, especially as religious chauvinism and expansionism has come to dominate its politics, has become a new kind of idolatry, deeply corrosive to Jewish values. As Peter Beinart writes in his brave and prophetic 2025 book, *Being Jewish After the Destruction of Gaza*, in both Israel and America, the state of Israel has been elevated to something like godhood. For starters, by law, political parties in Israel cannot oppose the existence of the State of Israel as a Jewish and democratic state. And, as Beinart writes, "Many American Jewish institutions also deem rejecting Jewish statehood the greatest possible sacrilege." Campus Hillel programs say they will welcome Jewish students regardless of their level or lack of religious observance, but speakers who "delegitimize" Jewish statehood are explicitly prohibited from speaking at Hillel. Speakers who delegitimize God are not prohibited. Beinart adds, "Treating a state as a god is a very frightening endeavor."[9]

Second, I believe that only a process of mutual recognition and reconciliation between Israelis and Palestinians, including the establishment of a Palestinian state beside Israel or some form of confederation, can heal the bitter wounds of war, dispersion, terrorism, and hatred. Third, in pursuit of this solution, I look for moderation in the Palestinian camp within the framework of Palestinian nationalism and expect moderation on the Israeli side within the framework of Zionism. To advocate anti-Zionism as the only solution is to me as bankrupt an idea as anti-Palestinianism. It gives me little solace to note that such are the mutually-reinforcing stands of both sides' leadership at the present. Though Jews are the oppressors today, I have not forgotten the oppression that my parents' generation (and many others before them) suffered because they were Jews. Thus, paraphrasing the Israeli Druze journalist Rafik Halabi, I believe one should regard the attitude of a Palestinian Arab toward the "Jewish problem" as the touchstone by which to judge his morality, and likewise view the attitude of an Israeli Jew toward the "Palestinian problem" as the test of his morality.

I would only add, to the degree that Zionism has become fully synony-

---

8. Shaul Magid, *The Necessity of Exile* (Ayin Press, 2023).
9. Peter Beinart, *Being Jewish After the Destruction of Gaza* (Alfred Knopf, 2025), pp. 102-3.

mous with Jewish supremacy in the land from the river to the sea, then I reject it and would call myself a post-Zionist or a non-Zionist. Perhaps it is time for those of us who want the fourteen million Israeli Jews and Palestinian Arabs who live there to be able to do so in peace, security and equality to set aside our obsession with Zionism, either as something we are passionately for or something we vehemently oppose. It's time to move past this binary way of thinking about the conflict, if we are ever to see it end.

If Israelis and Palestinians can learn to accept the legitimacy of each other's national narratives, can they also forge a shared future as well? That is the premise of A Land For All, a joint Israeli-Palestinian peace group founded in 2012 that has been developing a fresh approach to resolving the historic conflict. It suggests something different from the "two-state solution" that was supposed to be the product of the Oslo Accords of the early 1990s, but which now is a mirage. A Land for All's model envisions Israel-Palestine as a single territorial unit, with two sovereign and independent states linked by a porous border allowing for freedom of movement through an agreed mechanism whose implementation would be phased in over time with security restrictions imposed individually instead of collectively and unequally, as they are today. Instead of being divided by walls, each side would be able to cross these borders for tourism, study or work.

Key features of this model include joint mechanisms and institutions for shared concerns such as managing climate change and natural resources, as well as a shared economic zone to reduce the gap between Israelis and Palestinians, a joint Israeli-Palestinian court of human rights to resolve conflicts, Jerusalem as the capital of both states administered by a joint municipal council, and tight security collaboration while maintaining separate security forces for each state.

A Land for All also addresses the issue of Palestinian refugees and Israeli settlers, by allowing Palestinian refugees to return to Israel as citizens of Palestine, while Israeli settlers in Palestine could remain citizens of Israel as permanent residents in the other state, if they accept the sovereignty of that state and respect its laws and while dismantling any system of superiority or oppression.

While the details of how many Palestinians could move back to their former towns inside Israel and how many Israelis could stay in their current homes in the occupied West Bank would obviously have to worked out, one thing this vision recognizes is that paradoxically, many Palestinians have a great attachment to places inside pre-1967 Israel while many Israelis have a great attachment to places in what was once the Biblical Jewish heartland of Judea and Samaria. The organization specifically commits not to rectify one injustice with creating another as part of its commitment to reconciliation. I now think something like A Land for All is more realistic than the old "two-state solution," though to be clear, any of these compromises will require something like a cultural revolution among both Israelis and Palestinians akin to the generational shift that produced an end to Northern Ireland's "troubles." This is a daunting vision, but without vision, both peoples will perish.

As the *Pirke Avot* teaches, it is not up to us to finish this work, but we are also not at liberty to neglect it.

Micah L. Sifry, October, 2025

CHAPTER 1
THE "OFFICERS' LETTER"

THE POLITICAL BACKGROUND

Mr. Menachem Begin
   Prime Minister
   State of Israel

Mr. Prime Minister,
   This letter is sent to you by citizens of Israel who also serve as reserve officers and soldiers.
   It is with heavy hearts that we write these words to you. However, in these days when for the first time new vistas are opening up for the State of Israel, for a life of peace and cooperation in the region, we feel duty bound to call upon you to refrain from taking any steps that are liable to be a source of regret for generations to come, for our people and for our state.
   We write to you out of the deepest concern. A government that will prefer the existence of Israel in borders of the Greater Israel to its existence of peace in the context of good neighborly relations will arouse in us grave misgivings.
   A government that will prefer the establishment of settlements across the "green line" to the ending of the historic conflict and the establishment of a system of normal relations, will raise questions about the justice of our course. A government policy that will lead to the continued rule over one million Arabs is liable to damage

the Jewish democratic character of the state, and would make it difficult for us to identify with the basic direction of the state of Israel.

We are fully aware of the security requirements of the State of Israel and the difficulties that lie on the path to peace. Nonetheless, we know that true security will be achieved only with the advent of peace. The strength of the Israel Defense Forces lies in the identification of its soldiers with the course of the State of Israel.

We call upon you to choose the path of peace, and through this choice, to strengthen our faith in the justice of our cause.

(The Officers' Letter, March 7, 1978)

The publication of this letter, signed by 348 reserve officers and combat soldiers, triggered a massive and spontaneous outpouring of support for its message—an outpouring which became Shalom Ackshav, the Peace Now movement. In the months and years to follow, Peace Now became a dynamic factor in Israeli politics, mobilizing hundreds of thousands around the principles expressed in the Officers' Letter—protesting Begin's inflexibility in the negotiations with the Egyptians, the ongoing occupation of the West Bank and the Gaza Strip, and the war in Lebanon.

The real impact of the Officers' Letter cannot be understood, however, without examining the political background that led to its publication. The period from the spring of 1977 to the spring of 1978 was marked by four important developments: the election of Menachem Begin's Likud Party, the foundering of the proposed Geneva peace negotiations on the question of Palestinian representation, Egyptian President Anwar Sadat's visit to Jerusalem, and the difficulties in the Egyptian-Israeli negotiations.

Begin's rise to power capitalized on the long-ruling Labor Party's internal problems and affirmed the gradual shift to the nationalist right that had begun after the 1967 war in the perceived absence of a viable peace option. He inherited a settlement policy that was based on Labor's so-called Allon plan, which had called for building settlements along the Jordan River valley (avoiding West Bank population centers), in the Golan Heights, in the southern end of the Gaza strip, and in the Rafiah salient in northern Sinai. The land to be retained under this plan amounted to not only 40% of the total land area of the West Bank and Gaza, but 90% of all the arable land—including most of the water and natural resources. The Allon plan also called for the economic and administrative, though not legal or formal, integration of the occupied territories into Israel. Thus while the actions that Begin was to authorize did not create the whole problem of Israel's "creeping annexation" of the West Bank, they inaugurated a clear ideological shift in governmental policy toward the occupied territories.

More importantly, even before the establishment of Israel in 1948, Begin and his adherents, all disciples of Vladimir Jabotinsky's Revisionist Zionism, had espoused the Jewish people's inalienable right to all of Eretz Israel —"the Land of Israel"—then considered by them to include "both sides of the Jordan" (i.e. Transjordan as well) and later moderated to just "Western Eretz Israel" (i.e. pre-1967 Israel plus the West Bank). True to his word, Begin stated one week after his election victory:

"I believe Judea and Samaria [the biblical names for the West Bank] are an integral part of our sovereignty. It is our land. It was occupied by Abdullah [King of Jordan] against international law, against our inherent right. It was liberated during the Six Day War, when we used our right of national self-defense ... You annex foreign land. You don't annex your own country."[1]

Contrasted with the Labor Party's 1977 election platform, which had stated that "political efforts to reach permanent peace in defensible borders with Egypt, Jordan and Syria are to be continued with readiness for territorial compromise with each of them,"[2] this was a definite change, though not in respect to the question of Palestinian national rights.

On July 26, 1977, the Begin government formally approved three existing Jewish settlements on the West Bank that had been considered illegal and ineligible for governmental support by Labor. All three were near large Arab population centers and had been started by the religious nationalist group Gush Emunim ("Bloc of the Faithful"). This was the first concrete signal of Begin's convenient alliance with the ultra-nationalist right. Plans for three new settlements were approved on August 17, and on the second of September, hardline Agriculture Minister Ariel Sharon unveiled a master plan to settle "about two million Jews by the end of the

---

1. William Frankel, *Israel Observed: An Anatomy of the State*, p. 56.
2. Lester A. Sobel, ed., *Peace-Making in the Middle East*, p. 131.

century in a security belt stretching from the Golan Heights in the north to the tip of the Sinai Peninsula."[3]

Needless to say, these initiatives were condemned by the United States as "obstacles to peace." At the same time, U.S.-sponsored attempts to reconvene the Geneva peace conference kept running into obstacles—the core of which pertained to Israeli refusals to allow the participation of Palestine Liberation Organization representatives in the negotiations. The most notable of developments during this period were the gradual shift in U.S. policy towards favoring a "homeland" for the Palestinians and guaranteeing their "legitimate rights."

On both the Syrian and Egyptian fronts, Israel appeared willing to trade territories for peace, but no Arab leader was willing to grant Israel a separate peace to the detriment of the Palestinians. In the final analysis there was just one intractable problem: the gap between the Israeli proposal to grant the West Bank and Gaza Strip Arabs internal autonomy while maintaining Israeli sovereignty, and the Arab-backed P.L.O. demand for an independent state in Palestine. As later events have shown, this remains one of the central obstacles to peace.

Sadat's visit to Israel upended the status quo. One Peace Now leader, Omri Padan, later remarked that "The big shock was Sadat's visit. Until then I had doubts—maybe there really is no one to talk to in the Arab world. Maybe I am wrong. Sadat's visit changed everything."[4] As Sadat himself said in his speech to the Israeli Knesset, "In all sincerity I tell you we welcome you among us with full security and safety. This in itself is a tremendous turning point, one of the landmarks of a decisive historical change."[5]

One public opinion poll in Israel showed that during Sadat's visit the proportion of "Israelis who 'definitely believe' or 'believe' that Egypt is interested in peace" doubled from the usual range of 40 to 50% to 91%.[6] The parallel jump that took place in Israeli perceptions of the other Arab countries' interest in peace, measured by the same poll, indicated a general shift in Israeli attitudes. From this point on, it would become a little bit

---

3. Ibid., pp 148- 150.
4. *Ha'aretz*, March 31, 1978.
5. Sobel, ed., op. cit., p. 173.
6. Russell A. Stone, *Social Change in Israel: Attitudes and Events, 1967-1979*, p. 32.

harder for Israeli politicians to simply blame the Arabs for the continuation of the state of war.

The last precipitating factor in the rise of Peace Now was the impasse in the Egyptian-Israeli negotiations that followed and the perception of many Israelis that Begin's inflexibility was to blame. Begin offered Sadat a peace plan that would give the residents of Judea, Samaria and the Gaza Strip "administrative autonomy," but reserved sovereignty, the right to settle, and responsibility for security to Israel.[7] Sadat's response was to reaffirm his commitment to a total Israeli withdrawal from the occupied territories (including settlements) and Israeli recognition of the right of their Arab residents to self-determination in exchange for iron-clad security arrangements for Israel. Israeli desires to retain its northern Sinai settlements became another sticking point. On January 8, 1978, the Israeli cabinet barred the creation of new settlements in the Sinai, but it approved the expansion of the 20 existing ones and urged more Israelis to move there.[8]

These disagreements led to the breakdown of talks on January 18, when Sadat recalled the Egyptian delegation to the Political Committee the two countries had set up. In response to critical statements by Sadat, Begin decided on January 22 to delay resuming Israeli participation in the parallel Military Committee negotiations. These talks resumed at the end of January but recessed without any formal announcement.

Meanwhile, returning to the Zionist habit of "creating facts on the ground," four new settlements were established on the West Bank in mid-January, including one at a site called Shiloh that was ostensibly an "archeological dig," but was occupied by 25 families from Gush Emunim. The Labor opposition and the Israeli press objected to the damage these actions did to Israel's credibility during the negotiations with Egypt, and Washington repeated its criticism of the settlements as obstacles to peace. Despite these internal and external pressures, the Israeli cabinet decided on February 26 to maintain its settlement policy. Only Defense Minister Ezer Weizman appeared to regard the Sinai settlement activity as politically harmful.

Such were the political developments that set the stage for the appear-

---

7. Sobel ed., op. cit., p. 188.
8. Ibid., p. 198.

ance of the Officers' Letter and the creation of the Peace Now movement. The resurrection and popularization of the "doves" in Israel was, of course, not a purely spontaneous occurrence. Behind it was a small but determined group of young men and women—most of them students at the Hebrew University in Jerusalem.

THE ROOTS OF PEACE NOW

Peace Now actually had its roots in a small group that called itself the "Movement for a Different Zionism" (Ha'Tnua La'Zionut Acheret). According to Amos Arieli, one of its founders, this group came into existence "two weeks after the election when we heard that Begin is the Prime Minister and the Likud is the government and that Eretz Israel Hashlemah ["the Greater Land of Israel"] is part of the program of the government."[9] In its ideology and goals the group was strikingly similar to Peace Now. An information sheet they put out spoke of their concern about growing Israeli extremism, and sought a "broad, supra-party public activity to counter [it] and to create an atmosphere in which steps leading to real peace will be welcomed." They emphasized their identification with Israel as a Jewish democratic state, and condemned the occupation harshly, saying:

> "Rule over the Arab people in the territories who have their own national aspirations, in essence compulsion does not be the existence of democratic rule and is liable to corrupt and weaken our moral strength. Application of the concept that our security depends on permanent holding of the territories is liable to prolong the state of war and prevent a peaceful solution."[10]

According to Arieli, the group had about 200 active members and about 1,000 supporters in total, mostly centered in or around the Hebrew University in Jerusalem. It held a few demonstrations during the fall of 1977, but

---

9. Susan Elsen, *Shalom Achshav—The Peace Now Movement in Israel: A Bus on the Road to Peace*, unpublished senior thesis, History Department, Princeton University, April 18, 1979; interview with Amos Arieli, October 24, 1978, quoted on p. 69. I am indebted to Elsen for this early spadework on the movement's origins.
10. *New Outlook*, September 1977, p. 61.

attracted little attention.[11] Ariel Rubenstein, a member of the Movement for a Different Zionism and later one of the authors of the Officers' Letter, recalled that for the group Sadat's visit was "a fork in the road ... After Sadat we organized three or four little demonstrations and we had meetings, but we felt that something had changed and we felt that it was time [for] a great movement and not a little movement [like] Zionut Acheret."[12]

The months after Sadat's historic visit were a time of great frustration for the future leaders of Peace Now. Yoram Kribin spoke of his despair and anguish as "a feeling of weakness—a kind of worthlessness, as if you are just a small pawn ... I always thought that the government of Israel would always try to find every chance for peace, and then I saw it was [slipping] out of our hands, step by step ... You start asking yourself questions."[13]

Many of these men had volunteered for difficult and dangerous posts in the army out of a sense of idealism. Their faith in the justice of Israel's position was very important to them. Abu Vilan, a burly dairy farmer from Kibbutz Negba who was one of Peace Now's key organizers, told me that, "After thirty years [of hearing] 'nobody to talk to' and 'the Arab understands only force', and here for the first time was a real alternative. And we had a deep feeling that maybe ... three or four months after the historic visit of President Sadat ... this government was going to miss this chance."[14]

The weakness and disarray of the Labor opposition was also a factor in politicizing previously inactive Israelis. Said Yiftach Ya'acov, another Peace Now activist in Jerusalem: "The peace negotiations were dying, the world was pointing an accusing finger at us, and you look around and ask: 'Where is the labor movement?' 'Where is the sane leadership?' 'Where did the people of the kibbutz movement disappear to?' ...So you pace your house like a wounded deer, bang your head on the wall, and [finally] decide to get up ... in order to do something."[15]

But what could they do? In their work in the Movement for a Different Zionism, they had discovered that many people refused to even listen to

---

11. Elsen, op. cit., interview with Amos Arieli, quoted on p. 70.
12. Ibid., interview with Ariel Rubenstein, November 5, 1978, quoted on p. 71.
13. Ha'aretz, March 31, 1978.
14. Author interview with Abu Vilan, August 5, 1982.
15. Ha'aretz, March 31, 1978.

their message. Amos Arieli described how they were dismissed in the typical encounter: "The people in Zionut Acheret, most of them, were officers or soldiers in the front lines, and what people said to us was 'Ah, you think so [that peace is better than Greater Israel] because you are not in the Army, because you never fought.' They didn't want to hear what we said— the arguments were not if we were right or wrong, [rather] - 'you don't have the right to speak, you are traitors.'"[16]

In a very real way, they were nearly powerless. Moti Perry, another author of the Officers' Letter and a pilot in the Israeli air force who was studying at the Hebrew University at the time, said, "I, and I'm sure many other people, [felt] very bad at this time. You feel that maybe it's the last chance and the one chance for Israel to make peace in the Middle East, and you see that our government is losing this chance, and you don't know what to do." He paused and sighed. "Sometimes you [watch] the TV and you want to shout, [but] you feel that you are just one [person]."

Perry said that he remembered one night when he couldn't sleep from the torment he felt. "I remember I told Yuval [Neriah] and Ariel [Rubenstein] 'if we continue to study, we [won't be able to] explain it to our children [for] all of our lives and we [won't be able to] to forgive ourselves ... ' We always thought about it, but we really didn't know what to do because we were just 5, 10, 20 students at the University with no money, nothing ... and then came the idea of the Officers' Letter."[17]

The idea itself originated in a telephone conversation between Moti Perry and his twin brother Meir, who lived on Kibbutz Yad Mordechai. Earlier, a group of high school students from Beersheva had sent Begin a letter expressing their difficulty preparing to be drafted into the army, given the direction of his policies. Such initiatives were always easily dismissed as "defeatist" or "naïve." A letter signed by officers and members of elite units would be a more powerful but riskier step, for in Israel the army has traditionally remained apart from politics.

But the time was urgent. "When we saw that ... peace was going to disappear," said Amos Arieli, "We thought that maybe we will sign an officers' letter ... [then] people couldn't say to us 'you are traitors' ... they

---

16. Elsen, op. cit., interview with Amos Arieli, quoted on p. 72.
17. Ibid., interview with Moti Perry, November 15, 1978.

[would] have to respond to what we [were] saying, they wouldn't be able to just ignore us."[18] More importantly, Moti Perry, told me a few years later at Princeton University, where he was pursuing a graduate degree, "We wanted to show that you can be a patriot, a Zionist, and still criticize ... that being a Zionist does not mean being Gush Emunim." He added, "We had to do it—it was burning inside us."[19]

Initially, Perry, Rubenstein and Yuval Neriah (a Yom Kippur War hero and university student) each tried to draw up a draft of the letter. After a great deal of arguing and nitpicking, a friend of Perry's who was on his way to becoming a lawyer, Tzali Reshef, synthesized a version acceptable to the group. Reshef was to prove to have an excellent sense of strategy and came to be a key leader of the movement. He later commented on the letter: "We tried to give a hidden threat. It was not really a threat, but it was to tell the government to pay attention to the phenomenon that people who are serving in the combat units ... who are going to pay the price [of another war] ... What I was trying to [say was] 'look, these are people of [integrity], you can't just ignore them. They are not defeatists, they are not leftists or haters of Israel ... It was the fact that we used this gimmick, I would say, that was something that gave a lot of power to the movement."[20]

None of the letter's signers were seriously suggesting that in the next war they would not fight, as Omri Padan later told Ha'aretz, Israel's highly respected leftwing daily newspaper. "If war breaks out, I want that a soldier will get into his 'Zelda' [armored personnel carrier] at one with himself ... that [he] will know that we did everything possible to prevent a war ... It will be a very hard feeling to go to war knowing it could have been prevented. Israel always claims that her secret weapon is the Israel Defense Force's spirit ... that there is no other choice ... Don't get me wrong ... all of us here will fulfill our duty in every case, but the doubts will be very hard to remove."[21]

With ten core people, the group quickly gathered over 300 hundred signatures—among them about one-third were kibbutzniks, more than 250

18. Ibid., interview with Amos Arieli, quoted on p. 73.
19. Author interview with Moti Perry, January-February 1983.
20. Elsen, op. cit., interview with Tzali Reshef, November 13, 1978, quoted on p. 75.
21. Ha'aretz, March 31, 1978.

were lieutenants and captains, 15 were majors and two were lieutenant generals.[22] The presence of Yuval Neriah's name gave the movement real credibility, for he was one of the few living recipients of Israel's 'Itur Hagvura', the country's highest award for valor and the equivalent of the British Victoria Cross or the Congressional Medal of Honor. For the most part the group was ill-prepared for the storm they unexpectedly unleashed. Moti Perry told the *Jerusalem Post* that they had hoped the letter might act as a "catalyst ... to shock the kibbutz movement and Labor" into doing something.[23]

In early March they quickened their efforts collecting signatures because Begin was to leave for the U.S. soon and they wanted him to receive the letter before he left. As Dedi Zucker, another important Peace Now leader, remarked to me when we met in Jerusalem in August of 1982, "Nobody had any idea of what they were getting into."[24] Two days before the letter's publication, they told a few journalists. "Then we saw it was going to boom just by their reaction," Moti Perry recalled over one of our coffee meetings in Princeton. "It was the first time I was worried." The night before, Professor Yehoshua Arieli, Amos' father and a key figure in the dovish Movement for Peace and Security that had formed after the 1967 war, came to them with a lawyer and begged them not to release the letter because he feared they would be jailed. That night the ten of them sat together. Perry said that "We knew it was going to be big and [we were] a little bit afraid."[25]

The letter clearly struck a chord in Israeli society, provoking a reaction the group was totally unprepared for: people turned to them for guidance and leadership. "The telephone wouldn't stop ringing," said Perry. "People were asking 'what do you want us to do—how can we help you?" He remembers that at first, they had no idea what to suggest, "and then someone from Haifa called and said he had put a table outside his house and started collecting signatures supporting the letter, and he wanted to send them to us. So we started telling people who were calling to collect

---

22. Arieh Palgi, *Shalom Ve' Lo Yoteir* (Peace and No More), p. 22.
23. *Jerusalem Post*, July 27, 1979.
24. Author interview with Dedi Zucker, August 18, 1982.
25. Author interview with Moti Perry, January-February 1983.

signatures." In just a few days, over 5000 were collected in Haifa alone.[26] Over 100,000 signatures were collected in only two months in this manner, despite attempts by Gush Emunim members to disrupt some of the petition tables.

The weeks following the letter's release were a period of intense discussion and activity for the group. At first some people hesitated. After a frustrating experience with the Movement for a Different Zionism, doing "enormous" amounts of work with few results, some people were skeptical. Perry told me that, "Most of our time was spent arguing among ourselves —are we personally strong enough to go on?"[27] Yet everyone knew they had to try.

Three days after the letter was published, a group in Tel Aviv published an ad in the daily *Ha'aretz*, calling upon the "silent majority" to speak out and "not allow a fanatical minority to write our future."[28] Momentum was building even without the intervention of the letter's initiators in Jerusalem. (Incidentally, the group in Tel Aviv was actually the first to use the name Shalom Ackshav—Peace Now, a name that eventually stuck despite a later effort to change it to the less brash-sounding "Movement for Peace").

The following Saturday, the Jerusalem group met at Tzali Reshef's house, where it was suggested that they do a demonstration in Tel Aviv to test the political waters. That same night, a Palestinian terrorist raid on the coastal road occurred, in which 27 Israelis were killed and 70 injured. The nation mourned. Fearful of being branded by the government as supporters of the Palestine Liberation Organization (P.L.O.), the group placed an ad in *Ha'aretz* addressed "to the Palestinians" and stating that "organizations of murder and terror are taking you, by their deeds, out of the family of nations ... Don't let extremists bring the two peoples down the path of no return."[29] In a seemingly naive but deliberate way, this message attempted to evoke an image of two peoples willing to coexist, but led astray by their leaders. It clearly had the intended effect on the Israeli public, for support for the embryonic movement continued to grow.

---

26. *Jerusalem Post*, April 14, 1978.
27. Author interview with Moti Perry, January-February 1983.
28. *Ha'aretz*, March 10, 1978.
29. *Ha'aretz*, March 13, 1978.

A week later, at a national meeting in Jerusalem of groups and interested people from around the country, the decision to organize a demonstration was made. Speaking a few years later, Abu Vilan told me he remembered the discussion this way: "We decided we have nothing to lose ... if they [the public] don't come, so [at least] we did a letter and maybe the public isn't prepared [for it] or doesn't want it ..."[30] They spoke of 5,000 people as a successful turnout. Plans were made to print 10,000 postcards for people to sign and send to Prime Minister Begin. Abu Vilan helped bring the support of the Kibbutz Artzi movement—the federation of kibbutzim affiliated with the left-wing Mapam party. The Kibbutz Artzi movement provided them with some initial funds, which were later paid back, and logistical help with the preparations for the demonstration, scheduled for the first of April. Two days beforehand, they held a press conference announcing the beginning of a "public struggle."[31]

30. Author interview with Abu Vilan, August 5, 1982.
31. *Jerusalem Post*, March 30, 1978.

CHAPTER 2
THE FIGHT FOR PEACE
WITH EGYPT

PEACE NOW'S first big rally that early April Saturday night in Tel Aviv was a success beyond anyone's expectations, and really marked the birth of mass protest politics in Israel. Between thirty and forty thousand people came.[1] "You have to understand that, then, for an Israeli political demonstration," Abu Vilan explained to me, "the biggest one had been 15,000 to 20,000 for Gush Emunim, and on the dovish side 15,000 at the largest."[2] The event was widely covered by the Israeli and world media. *Jerusalem Post* correspondent Helga Dudman commented on the young and abnormally well-behaved crowd: "The air was, I should say, thick with idealism. Which may be another way of saying that it was thick with non-realism. On the other hand, who is to say that soldiers are unrealistic?"[3]

Hundreds held placards reading "Security, not settlements," "Zionist values, not territories," "Flexibility requires courage," and "Don't ruin the chance for peace." According to a *Ha'aretz* poll published March 30, 55.1% of the population feared that new settlements would hurt the chances for peace.[4]

With a gleam in his eyes, Moti Perry reminisced to me about the early

---

1. *Jerusalem Post*, April 4, 1978.
2. Author interview with Abu Vilan, August 5, 1982.
3. *Jerusalem Post*, April 5, 1978
4. *Ha'aretz*, March 30, 1978.

days of Peace Now: "It was very exciting ... for years you see what's happening and you want to scream—'What's is going on in my country? Where are the people?' You feel helpless and then in two weeks you feel you have the power to change something. Thousands of people are ready to help ... we had volunteers all over the country. I didn't do anything else." He added, "It was fun to meet every night together," speaking of the core group in Jerusalem. "We went through very difficult but also very exciting times." He also admitted that as college students—albeit more mature than 18-year-olds because of their army and reserve service—they wondered if they were capable of the task ahead.[5]

Did they consider if they were a representative group that could reach all sectors of Israeli society? Clearly not. Such is the challenge with movements that arise from semi-spontaneous action combined with intense media attention: people are thrust into roles that they have no preparation for, but to the outside world they are expected to perform the equivalent of political organizing magic.

Building on the demonstration's tremendous success, organizers around the country met a week later, on April 7, to officially found the "Movement for Peace" under two slogans: "Peace Now" and "Peace is Better than a Greater Israel." The former was the choice of the Tel Avivites, who tended to prefer a bolder approach, while the latter was preferred by the Jerusalem group and the kibbutzniks, because it better expressed the movement's sensibility.

From the start, it was agreed that the movement was to be strictly volunteer—no one was to get paid. This was to maintain the movement's idealistic purity and spontaneity in the face of natural tendencies toward bureaucracy and vested interests, but it was to take its toll in the eventual fatigue and burn-out of key people. A few standing committees were set up to deal with finances, connections with the diaspora (Jews from abroad), and press releases. Actions were to be planned and executed on an ad-hoc basis, by people who volunteered to take responsibility for them.

It was also agreed that the different regional circles of activists would not take unilateral initiatives, and that they would appoint representatives to a national forum to coordinate activities. Lastly, it was agreed to

---

5. Author interview with Moti Perry, January-February 1983.

centralize the collection and spending of funds to also facilitate organizational unity.[6] For all intents and purposes, real decision-making power rested in the hands of the original Jerusalem core group, and outside of general agreement on the principles described in the Officers' Letter, little was resolved in the realm of policy or strategy. These topics of leadership, organizational process and strategy will be returned to in Chapter Seven.

The initial reaction of the Begin government to the Officers' Letter was far from positive. At first, attempts were made to discredit it. In a short amount of time, however, the government realized that Peace Now represented a serious threat—and eventually it came to view the movement as its most significant adversary. Finance Minister Simcha Ehrlich of the Liberal Party, a junior member of the government coalition, reacted with suspicion, saying that a movement founded by a group of reserve officers "smells of a putsch." Apparently, Peace Now's rapid rise in popularity was viewed with enough apprehension in government circles to warrant the creation of a "spontaneous" "popular" counter-movement.

This counter-efforts, calling itself the "Movement for a Secure Peace," was launched on April 6, and by April 9 claimed that it had collected 132,000 signatures supporting the government's peace policy. Its spokesman, Hanan Abramson, denied that the movement had been initiated by any party or political bloc. To his chagrin, evidence began to surface pointing to connections between this group and the ruling parties and the Gush Emunim movement.[7] When only between thirty and forty thousand people showed up at their April 15 rally in Tel Aviv and not the widely expected number of 100,000 or more, the Movement for a Secure Peace faded into non-existence after sponsoring a few petitions.[8]

Reactions from the Israeli political leadership were mixed. Begin's first response to the Officers' Letter was to ask its authors if they accepted his position, or therefore agreed with the "ultimate demands of the Arabs to withdraw to the 1967 borders and accept a Palestinian state." They replied that there was a middle position, based on a non-ideological concern for Israel's security. When a promised meeting between Begin and three Peace

---

6. Author interview with Abu Vilan, August 5, 1982.

7. *Jerusalem Post*, April 6, 1978; April 17, 1978; April 21, 1978; and Yehonatan Tommer, "Peace Now: Popular Protest in Israel," *The World Today*, July 1978, p. 250.

8. *Jerusalem Post*, April 16, 1978 and April 19, 1978.

Now representatives—Yuval Neriah, Omri Padan and Moti Perry—finally took place on April 21, he reiterated his stand.

"It was a boring conversation," Perry recalled years later. "Nothing new was said."[9] The three men argued for a willingness for territorial compromise on the West Bank and Begin countered that his autonomy plan was the best solution. He tried to argue that others in their army units favored his position by showing them letters of support that he had received, and Neriah responded that "in my unit 90% have signed the Officers' Letter.[10] Padan likened Begin's position to that of Gush Emunim, and Begin replied by noting that taking a strong stance had probably served Israel well in its dealings with the U.S. over the question of a Palestinian state.[11]

In essence, Begin presented the Peace Now representatives with the same inflexible stands that President Carter had outlined as obstacles after his meeting with Begin a month earlier: refusal to relinquish the Sinai settlements, refusal to halt West Bank settlement activity, and denial of the applicability of U.N. Resolution 242's call for Israeli withdrawals from captured territories in the West Bank.[12]

A meeting a day earlier with Deputy Prime Minister Yigal Yadin of the new Democratic Movement for Change party, a more centrist member of Begin's governing coalition, went better for the Peace Now activists. Yadin agreed to support them if they would clarify their stand in a detailed manner that was consistent with his party's platform. They, in turn, suggested he resign from the government to fight for his views, which were considerably more moderate than Begin's, but he replied that he felt he could do more inside the government.[13]

This encounter presaged the beginning of the Democratic Movement for Change's break-up over the peace issue. Many informed observers had noted the similarities in the background of supporters of the D.M.C., and later, of Peace Now. Born as a reform party interested in transforming the electoral system, and supported by the votes of disillusioned Laborites, the D.M.C.'s star started to fade as soon as Yadin joined the Begin government

9. Author interview with Moti Perry, January-February 1983.
10. Ibid.
11. *Jerusalem Post*, April 23, 1978.
12. Sobel, ed., op. cit., p. 202.
13. *Jerusalem Post*, April 21, 1978; May 2, 1978.

while compromising on the need for electoral reform. Begin's ideological leanings clashed with the positions of many of the D.M.C. 's members of Knesset, eventually leading to their desertion of the coalition.

Other key government ministers were less sympathetic to Peace Now. In a talk he gave April 16 at a meeting of a Likud faction, Foreign Minister Moshe Dayan attacked Peace Now for supposedly demanding an immediate agreement with the Arabs on Sadat's terms.[14] Peace Now representatives tried to convince Simcha Ehrlich, in a meeting with him, to publicly fight for his reportedly dovish views on territorial concessions on the West Bank. In reply he said, "I'm not prepared to express myself on this topic because it would weaken the government's stand in the negotiations." He accused them of weakening Israel by creating the impression that Israel was divided, a theme that was to crop up again and again in attacks on Peace Now.[15]

Speaking to an audience at the Technion University in Haifa, Agriculture Minister Ariel Sharon said he "welcomed" the debate on the peace issue, but also asserted that Peace Now was encouraging the Egyptians to hold out for more concessions from Israel. He reserved his sharpest criticism for "the political body behind Peace Now," accusing them of "trying to foster disunity as a result of their frustration at having lost power" and of seeking "to regain the power they lost last year."[16] It is worth noting that this statement was only a few steps away from the accusations of "treason" and "treachery" that Likud politicians showered on Labor in the last months of the 1981 election a few years later, inciting many to anti-Labor violence and vandalism.

Support for Peace Now's goals was forthcoming in various degrees from the other end of the political spectrum. On April 19, ten members of Knesset published a letter supporting Peace Now. They included the D.M.C.'s David Golomb and Mordecai Wirshubski, former foreign ministers Abba Eban and Yigal Allon, and Uzi Baram, Chaika Grossman, Menahem Hacohen, Haim Bar-Lev and Yossi Sarid (all from the Labor Party) and Shulamit Aloni (Citizens Rights Movement).[17] Shimon Peres,

---

14. *Jerusalem Post*, April 16, 1978.
15. *Jerusalem Post*, May 9, 1978.
16. *Jerusalem Post*, April 21, 1978.
17. *Jerusalem Post*, April 21, 1978.

then the Labor Party's leader, agreed that his party's platform and Peace Now's principles did not contradict each other.[18]

Though these statements produced no surprises or major converts to Peace Now, they accomplished their basic goal of bringing the movement additional publicity. At the same time, Peace Now activists were very busy organizing to broaden their public support and potential influence on the government. One tactic used was letters of support from prominent groups of Israelis. Many were actually initiated by Peace Now activists themselves in order to create, as Moti Perry described, "the atmosphere that the whole country is bubbling."[19]

It was through his initial efforts in garnering the support of a few important academics, for example, that 350 "Professors for Peace" called on Begin on May 23 to recognize that the slogan "A Secure Peace" under which he operated was misleading and would not lead to peace "but rather to the loss of friends, to the increased isolation of Israel in the international arena and the division of world Jewry.[20] A similar letter signed by 300 members of the Jewish religious community urged Begin to recognize that "the holiness of the land does not conflict with our aspiration for peace with the Arabs on the basis of reasonable compromise."[21] Clearly, this letter was intended to dispel the impression that the religious community was united behind Gush Emunim. A small group of religious doves called "Oz V'Shalom" (Courage and Peace) acted as a thorn in the side of the religious nationalists, occasionally participating in Peace Now activities and endowing its criticisms with added legitimacy.

The public support of many industrialists, bankers and business executives was another important accomplishment. Among the signers of a letter of support embracing the Officers' Letter were David Moshevitz, head of Elite Chocolate; the Head of the Polgat complex, Yekutiel Federman; and Naftali Blumenthal, Director General of Koor Industries, the Histadrut's industrial giant.[22] These industrialists provided significant financial support to Peace Now and also helped dispel the "leftist" and "idealist"

---

18. *Jerusalem Post*, May 26, 1978.
19. Author interview with Moti Perry, January-February 1983.
20. Elsen, op. cit., p. 66.
21. Ibid., p. 66.
22. Boaz Evron, "The New Israeli Peace Movement," *New Outlook*, September 1978.

labels that had been pinned on the movement. Also significant was the unsolicited arrival of a telegram supporting Peace Now from 37 prominent American Jews.[23] The movement's role among Diaspora Jewry was to become quite a controversial issue.

"We intended to mobilize people ... but we didn't know how. I didn't have any master plan, or list of practical things that should be done," Dedi Zucker later told me, commenting on the political inexperience of the movement's founders. One reason Peace Now held big regional meetings at the beginning of May was, as he said, "to ask people to suggest ideas."[24] From the approximately 4000 people who attended these meetings, including 1000 from Jerusalem, they were able to put together a telephone network which would later be very useful in mobilizing people on short notice. The movement began sending people to schools to give talks, setting up public forums, and convening neighborhood meetings in people's homes. Yet, despite its political inexperience, the Peace Now movement in its early days proved very capable at organizing creative and colorful protests that had the effect of strengthening their youthful and sincere image while at the same time effectively publicizing their concerns.

DEMONSTRATING FOR PEACE

The first of these demonstrations was called Operation "Prisat Shalom" ("the spreading of peace"). On April 26, some 4000 to 5000 people formed a human chain along a 15-mile stretch of the Tel Aviv Jerusalem highway, all wearing black and red Peace Now signs printed in Hebrew and English. Hand to hand, they passed 57,000 signed postcards and petitions all the way to the Prime Minister's Office in Jerusalem. At one point, Begin himself drove by the youthful gathering on his way to Tel Aviv. He could not help seeing the demonstrators along the highway. Although some

---

23. The letter was organized by Leonard Fein, the editor of *Moment* magazine. Signers included Nobel Prize winners Saul Bellow and Kenneth Arrow; noted intellectuals Daniel Bell, Irving Howe, Seymour Martin Lipset, Martin Peretz, and Leon Wieseltier; and leaders from major Jewish organizations like Albert Vorspan of the Reform movement and Ira Silverman of the American Jewish Committee. Linda Charlton, "37 Jews in U.S. Applaud Israelis Who Urged Flexibility on Peace," *The New York Times*, April 21, 1978.
24. Author interview with Dedi Zucker, August 18, 1982.

passing drivers voiced opposition, a large number responded positively. It was, as the *Jerusalem Post*'s reporter described, one of Israel's "most original, good-natured and orderly demonstrations in years," and it got much media coverage in Europe and the U.S. as well as in Israel.

Meanwhile, the Egyptian-Israeli talks continued to flounder. A visit by Defense Minister Ezer Weizman to Cairo March 30-31 failed to revive them. The future of the West Bank remained the main bone of contention. As if to add insult to injury, Weizman submitted a revamped West Bank settlement plan on May 17 that called for the completion of a new settlement started a month earlier. Weizman's plan also called for expanding five other existing settlements. Under the proposal, the six settlements would be developed as urban centers and would be Israel's last on the West Bank. It was hoped that 38,000 families would eventually move into the six cities, augmenting the existing Jewish population of 4,500 civilians.[25]

In response, Peace Now held a protest vigil outside the Prime Minister's Office. About 1,000 people participated in a demonstration that was marked by the presence of a "golden calf" effigy covered with slogans reading "The territories are the golden calf of Gush Emunim." Ministers leaving the weekly cabinet meeting were greeted with shouts of "Better peace than a greater Israel" and "Down with the annexation." Peace Now spokesman Tzali Reshef called for a national debate on the connection between territory and security and attacked the blind attachment to land for its own sake.[26] Between 5,000 and 8,000 people came to a nighttime rally in Haifa the next week.[27]

After these actions, Peace Now turned its attention to the Knesset, hoping to bring its message home to Israel's center of power. During the holiday of Shavuot, they held Operation "Shabbat Shalom," setting up 300 stations around the country to give out leaflets and collect signatures on an appeal to the government for moderation. This move was timed to hopefully influence the cabinet as it turned to consider a questionnaire sent from President Carter on Israel's stance regarding the future status of the

---

25. Sobel, ed., op. cit., p. 201.
26. *Jerusalem Post*, May 22, 1978.
27. Palgi, op. cit., p. 10.

West Bank and its preferred mechanism for achieving that status.[28] Two days later, 19 personal letters were sent by Peace Now to each of the members of the cabinet, emphasizing their historic opportunity and responsibility.[29]

Predictably, the cabinet opposed any suggestion of territorial conces-sion. It did, however, cautiously support the idea that after a five-year autonomy period, "the nature of the future relations between the parties will be considered and agreed upon" by Israel and the elected representa-tives of the West Bank and Gaza. Only Ezer Weizman and the four members of the Democratic Movement for Change opposed the cabinet resolution. It was approved by a 59-37 vote in the Knesset, with 10 members of the D.M.C. abstaining.[30] In a surprise protest, 15 Peace Now members disrupted the Knesset debate by standing up and revealing T-shirts emblazoned with the now-familiar "Peace is better than a Greater Israel."[31] Their action got wide media coverage.

They topped off this series of protests with a 5,000-person "peace siege" around the government offices in Jerusalem. Speakers attacked the govern-ment's replies to the American questionnaire as negative and called on Begin to resign to allow "others to make peace" if he could not.[32]

According to the accounts of government insiders, the only tangible impact that the Peace Now protests made on the governing coalition was the indirect strengthening of the D.M.C.'s moderate stand. Ezer Weizman's opposition to Begin's policies seemed more based in his assessment of Sadat's intentions. For example, he pointed to Sadat's mild rejection of the cabinet resolution as evidence that Sadat "is sincere" in his desire for peace.[33] The negotiations, however, remained stalled.

Israeli-Egyptian relations soured still further with the Israeli cabinet's rejection of a long-requested Egyptian counter-proposal on the future of the occupied territories even before it was made official. The plan called on

---

28. *Jerusalem Post*, June 8, 1978; Eitan Haber, Ze'ev Schiff, Ehud Ya'ari, *The Year of the Dove*, p. 197.
29. Palgi, op. cit., p. 10.
30. Sobel, ed., op. cit, p. 205.
31. *Jerusalem Post*, June 20, 1978.
32. *Jerusalem Post*, June 27, 1978 and June 28, 1978.
33. Sobel, ed., op. cit., p. 207.

Israel to withdraw from the West Bank, East Jerusalem, and the Gaza Strip in a five-year period, turning transitional sovereignty over to Jordan and Egypt. Its military rule and settlements would be withdrawn, and after the five-year period the Arab residents would "be able to determine their own future."[34] The plan was in response to the earlier Israeli proposal of December 1977 offering administrative autonomy to the Palestinians that Egypt had rejected.

Israel's rejection of the Egyptian formula was based on several criticisms: that no mention of a peace treaty or U.N. Resolutions 242 and 338 was made, that no mention was made of compensating Jewish refugees who fled Arab lands, that it called for Israel's abandonment of East Jerusalem, and that it spoke of Palestinians determining their own future without the participation of others.[35] In many ways, it represented a hardening of the Egyptian position since the Ismalia talks of December, but was used primarily as a bargaining tactic by Sadat.

Early in July he softened his position slightly in a meeting with Weizman in Austria, offering to allow Israel to maintain a military presence in the West Bank after the transition period. But an Israeli leak of this offer soured the atmosphere once more.[36] Begin rejected Sadat's request for the return of El Arish and Mt. Sinai as a conciliatory gesture, refusing to give him something for nothing. The final breakdown in the negotiations occurred July 17-18 in England at a meeting of Dayan, Egyptian Foreign Minister Mohammed Ibrahim Kamel and U.S. Secretary of State Cyrus Vance.

During the negotiations, Dayan offered to soften the Israeli position on the future sovereignty of the West Bank and Gaza if Egypt accepted Israel's autonomy proposal, declared Israel's willingness for a peace treaty based on territorial compromise in the Sinai, but repeated its rejection of a withdrawal to the pre-1967 borders. The Egyptians maintained the position taken earlier that month by Sadat, calling for a complete Israeli withdrawal and even referred obliquely to the formation of a Palestinian army on the West Bank—positions clearly unacceptable to Israel. An American compro-

---

34. Ibid., p. 207.
35. Ibid., pp. 207-208.
36. Haber, et. al., op. cit., pp. 204-207.

mise proposal for a federation or confederation of Jordan, the West Bank and Gaza that would have prevented the establishment of a Palestinian state was accepted by Egypt but rejected by Israel. The talks ended with Dayan threatening to retract Israel's proposal regarding a general withdrawal from Sinai. Though Vance would announce to the press that the talks would continue, it was clear that an impasse had been reached. Eight days later Sadat expelled the Israeli military mission in Alexandria.[37]

During this period, the perception of Begin as the major obstacle to peace was strengthened by statements from Sadat and Labor Party leader Shimon Peres. Sadat met with Peres in Austria on July 9. When Begin attacked Peres in the Knesset for going over his head, Peres replied that Sadat had told him he wanted Israel to withdraw completely from the Sinai but that he was willing to permit Israel to retain some part of the West Bank. Peres attacked Begin's goal of holding all of the West Bank as a "recipe for isolation.[38] Whether this was a clever ploy by Sadat to use Peres to pressure Begin is unclear and perhaps irrelevant. (Egypt's willingness to accept the American proposal for a Jordanian option perhaps confirmed Sadat's statement to Peres.) The point is that Peres' revelation had the effect of portraying Begin as the extremist. After the negotiation impasse in England, Sadat accused Begin of blocking a peace accord, saying: "If Israel, as it has said for 30 years, is really for peace, there is only one obstacle— Begin. Peace can be established within hours."[39]

In response to Sadat's demands for total Israeli withdrawal from the occupied territories, and after the expulsion of the Israeli military mission, Begin said that Sadat "wants peace with Israel according to his conditions, but his conditions mean the destruction of Israel." Going beyond his usual stress on Israel's biblical links to Judea and Samaria, Begin asserted that they were vital to Israel's security.[40]

Apparently Begin's inability to propose a territorial compromise on the West Bank as a bargaining response to Sadat made him appear the more inflexible of the two leaders. Sadat, on the other hand, was constantly hinting at compromises in his meetings with Weizman and Peres. When

---

37. Ibid., pp. 209-213.
38. Sobel, ed., op. cit., p. 209.
39. Ibid., p. 211.
40. Ibid., pp. 211-212.

the impasse was reached, both Begin and Sadat had hardened their positions, but Begin looked the worse for it. His popularity within Israel had fallen from 80% support after Sadat's visit to Jerusalem to just 50% that summer.[41] Meanwhile, the percent of Israelis who believed that Sadat was ready for peace had risen from just 43% in March to 62% by the end of July.[42]

Peace Now continued its pressure on Begin all through the summer. One thousand people demonstrated outside Begin's home on July 24 when the impasse in the negotiations came to light.[43] Another 70 industrialists publicized their support for the movement the next day. Their next focus of action was a rumored government plan to establish new settlements on the West Bank. First, they engineered a poster blitz against the proposal, plastering the inside and outside of public buildings around the country. The action set off a series of queries and denials within the governing coalition, leaving the rumors unconfirmed.[44]

Three days later, the movement struck for the first time at the heart of the issue by demonstrating on the West Bank. In a secret operation conceived several weeks before and prepared with great care, several thousand Peace Now supporters were summoned by telephone to a rocky hillside near the controversial "archeological" settlement of Shiloh. There they watched as a twenty-one-foot-high monument designed by sculptor Yigal Tumarkin, entitled "Dovecote," was set in place and dedicated. The speakers all voiced the hope that the monument would remain after the settlement had gone, and that when peace came it would be a symbol of Arab-Israeli coexistence. The organizers of the demonstration had fooled the nearby Gush Emunim settlers into helping maintain the pre-placed concrete base of the statue by telling them that it was to be for a communications antenna. The military authorities were also caught off guard.

The entire action was a complete success for Peace Now, especially in light of the press coverage and the surprisingly large turnout at what was essentially an illegal demonstration in the occupied territories.[45] The whole

---

41. Haber, et. al., op. cit., p. 208.
42. Stone, op. cit., p. 32.
43. *Jerusalem Post*, July 25, 1978.
44. *Jerusalem Post*, August 10, 1978, and August 11, 1978.
45. *Jerusalem Post*, August 13, 1978.

series of protests was vindicated the next day, August 14, when the cabinet decided to suspend consideration of the establishment of the rumored settlements pending the outcome of the upcoming Camp David talks.[46] Peace Now had been right on target. (To this day, Tumarkin's monument still stands, but the settlers living there have adopted it as a "blessing and proof of the permanence of Jewish communities in Judea and Shomron," as one of them wrote in 2016. They've even paid for its upkeep.)[47]

The culmination of Peace Now's first stage came with a massive peace rally held on the eve of the Camp David summit. One hundred thousand Israelis from all walks of life came to call on Prime Minister Begin to be more flexible regarding the issue of territorial compromise. The massive turnout showed that there was no national consensus regarding the permanent occupation of Judea and Samaria. Moreover, it showed that Peace Now had become an important factor in Israeli politics.

There is evidence that suggests that this demonstration also helped soften Begin's position during Camp David. Abu Vilan cited to me an unpublished letter from Begin to novelist Amos Oz, written during the summit, in which Begin told of how the vast numbers of Israelis demonstrating in Tel Aviv's Kikar Malchei Yisrael that night would run through his mind as he considered the decisions before him.[48] Perhaps Peace Now did strengthen Begin's willingness to concede more for peace, particularly on the issue of the withdrawal of the settlements in Sinai.[49] By agreeing to refer the question to the Knesset, and then linking it to a general vote on the accord with Egypt, Begin made the choice clear: peace or settlements. The Knesset supported him by a vote of 84 to 19, with 17 abstentions, with most of the dissent coming from within Begin's own Likud party. Peace Now activists welcomed him at the airport, when he returned from the U.S., in support of his tough decision.

---

46. Sobel, ed., op. cit., p. 202.

47. Shlomo Toren, "When Peace Now came, saw and blessed Shiloh," The Blogs, *The Times of Israel*, July 14, 2016, https://blogs.timesofisrael.com/when-peace-now-came-saw-and-blessed-shiloh/.

48. *Jerusalem Post*, July 29, 1979; author interview with Abu Vilan, August 5, 1982.

49. Haber, et. al., op. cit., pp. 262-268.

EARLY IMPACT AND STRATEGY

What was accomplished by Peace Now in its first exhilarating months of existence? Professor Ze'ev Sternhell, one of Israel's leading historians, described its fundamental impact as the "breaking of the national consensus ... [on] the basic question of national existence." In an article in *Ha'aretz*, he stated that Peace Now represented "young and middle-aged people [who] are refusing to recognize the legitimacy of the new Zionist purpose ... control over Judea and Samaria." The significance of this for Israeli politics was plain, as Sternhell, argued, "For the first time from the beginning of Zionism, the national leadership will have to present itself before the citizenry and say honestly that they prefer to control Western Eretz Israel more than they want to arrive at a solution of the conflict ... that the gap between our national interests and the national interests of the Arabs is so deep that there is no chance for peace—not in this generation or in the ones to follow."[50]

Moreover, added Moti Perry, looking back with a few years' hindsight, Peace Now "created a new environment" in Israel. It was no longer a shame or treason to be a dove or to criticize Begin, and Israelis, especially young people, saw a real Zionist alternative to Gush Emunim.[51]

It can be argued that the appearance of Peace Now had the effect of strengthening doves both within the governing coalition and the opposition. Certainly it spurred Labor to try to generate a more effective parliamentary opposition. It also had the effect of forcing most of the Democratic Movement for Change to stick to its principles. Internal dissent in that party culminated in June 1978, when Transport Minister Meir Amit and M.K. Amnon Rubenstein engineered wide support for an internal policy paper on the negotiations that echoed many of the points of the Officers' Letter.[52] Ezer Weizman may have also seen Peace Now as an ally. Whether these shifts and popular pressure generated by Peace Now affected the government's decisions in significant ways is another question. At least we

---

50. *Ha'aretz*, May 10, 1978.
51. Author interview with Moti Perry, January-February 1983.
52. *Jerusalem Post*, June 2, 1978.

may say that it definitely influenced the cabinet's August decision to halt new settlements prior to Camp David.

Whatever their impact on Begin, the Peace Now activists hid a canny sense of political strategy behind their image of naive, well-intentioned citizens. They had a flair for choosing colorful and provocative vehicles for their protests, which had the effect of enhancing their popularity and attractiveness. Dedi Zucker described his understanding of the movement's strategy in an interview that fall. First, he said, they agreed to only focus on the issue of war and peace. Second, to always strive to be "mainstream" in tactics and language–"We are not left, I mean the movement is not left but representing the mainstream," he said. Third was to avoid aligning with any political party in order to stay above the fray. They wanted, he said, to be seen "to remain beautiful, pure, young and unspoiled ... working just because of emotional, pure reasons — we are not doing politics, we are just fighting for peace." Finally, he said, "We knew our role in the political system was limited ...We could just be a kind of reflection of public opinion, dovish public opinion. And we should stay not only one-dimensional, but also a kind of movement which is not ideological. We don't have to deal with ideology. We just have to support or to oppose specific and concrete steps of the government or of the opposition, it doesn't matter, or of the Americans or of the Egyptians."[53]

But this caginess, which was strategic, also led to criticisms, even sometimes from Peace Now's own supporters, that its position was too vague. Newspapers carried articles with titles like "Slogans don't make a peace pact" and "'Peace Now' - - and then what?" Leaders of the movement argued that there was no need for them to draw maps and make detailed proposals for the negotiations. Said one, "our job is to create an atmosphere."[54] They said their role was that of focusing pressure on the whole political framework —coalition and opposition—to break the negotiating stalemate.

However, after President Sadat claimed in a speech that many Israelis supported his demands for a full withdrawal to the 1967 borders and the establishment of a Palestinian state and based his remarks mainly on the

---

53. Elsen, op. cit., interview with Dedi Zucker, quoted on pp. 79-80.
54. Ha'aretz, July 28, 1978.

whole Peace Now phenomenon, Peace Now leaders saw the need to write Sadat informing him that they did not support the acceptance of such a diktat.[55] In another incident, when 100 reservists announced in August that they would not be able to defend or guard settlements in the West Bank and Gaza Strip because they were an expression of "annexationist aims," Peace Now quickly condemned their action, emphasizing that "military service is over and above any political debate. In both cases, had the movement done otherwise, its credibility as a responsible (i.e. loyal, Zionist) and democratic (i.e. not extra-legal) movement would have been badly hurt.[56]

In the final analysis, it seems that the wisdom of this strategy of concentrating on propounding the general principles of the Officers' Letter was self-evident. Moti Perry told me that celebrated novelist Amos Oz praised this decision, that they had been "smart enough to push them [the government] to the extreme, not to let them push us." As Perry pointed out, by "avoid[ing] fighting over things that aren't relevant now" the movement could successfully unite a broad segment of the Israeli public against the government's current policy or actions.[57] Opinion polls consistently showed that between 50 and 70% of the Israeli population was willing to cede some of the occupied territories for peace, with between 10-20% willing to return all of them.[58] The catch was that this broad-based approach limited the movement's ability to initiate activities or plan steps toward long-range goals, for such attempts would have subjected the movement to much internal strain. As later developments were to show, such steps were unavoidable. The question was not whether the leaders of the movement would be willing to take them, but whether their supporters would follow.

---

55. *Ha'aretz*, May 15, 1978.
56. *Jerusalem Post*, August 23, 1978.
57. Author interview with Moti Perry, January-February 1983.
58. Stone, op. cit., p. 41.

CHAPTER 3
BATTLING FOR THE WEST BANK

THE LEADERS of Peace Now knew that their work was far from finished after Camp David. In this respect they were more sophisticated than many of their supporters, who showed a marked drop of interest in Peace Now. "Most of the people were sure that...there would be peace and everything was solved," Dedi Zucker told me a few years later. "We were sure that there would be more to do."[1] Moti Perry was suspicious of the Camp David accords. He believed, with good reason, that Begin's strategy was "to bribe the Egyptians [by] giving them Sinai for a separate peace ... [it was] clear to us that it wouldn't work, that the important battle was still ahead."[2]

Their role seemed clear-cut. "As a result of the Camp David agreements," said Tzali Reshef in an interview in the fall of 1978, "the problems [which Peace Now addresses] will now be more specific. It will be more difficult to say the vague things we said in the Officers' Letter. I think we'll all the time have to take into consideration what we should say, what we shouldn't say, but our aims will be to get a solution on the West Bank, by

---

1. Author interview with Dedi Zucker, August 18, 1982.
2. Author interview with Moti Perry, January-February 1983.

making concessions on the West Bank, by giving up our sovereignty ... These will be the main things we'll struggle about."[3]

Reshef added that he expected that Israelis would follow them in this struggle. Another activist from Jerusalem, Naftali Raz, expected a decline in support: "Peace Now will not be able to organize 100,000 people in a demonstration in Tel Aviv as we did, but the public and the government in Israel will remember Peace Now as we were...We will be able, I hope ... to keep the good name of the movement as a movement that represents thousands even though the thousands will be less."[4]

Zucker, however, remained optimistic: "The solution of the conflict is a business of a few more years and we should act and work [to] oppose the hawkish element ... basically we still have the same role: to oppose or to support trends and attitudes and ideas in the political system."[5] Reshef also believed that their task would also be "educational," saying, "We have to make the public understand that there will be no peace settlement without making concessions also on the West Bank."[6]

The first intimations that there would be problems implementing the proposed autonomy plans surfaced right after the Camp David summit. It became clear that Israel and the U.S. had fundamentally different interpretations of the future of Israeli settlements on the West Bank. Begin claimed that he had pledged to freeze new settlement activity on the West Bank only for the three-month period during which Israel and Egypt were expected to conclude their peace treaty. President Carter asserted in response that he had actually dropped a demand during Camp David that existing settlements not be expanded in return for Begin's agreement to an effective five-year moratorium on new West Bank settlements.[7]

The issue remained unresolved in the letters exchanged between the three nations after Camp David. Begin then revealed his strategy for retaining Israeli sovereignty over the West Bank after the five-year transition period. In a talk with a Jewish group in New York, he argued that if, after that period, the Palestinians or the Jordanians made the same claim

3. Elsen, op. cit., interview with Tzali Reshef, quoted on p. 83.
4. Ibid., interview with Naftali Raz, November 6, 1978, quoted on p. 84.
5. Ibid., interview with Dedi Zucker, quoted on p. 85.
6. Ibid., interview with Tzali Reshef, quoted on p. 85.
7. Sobel, ed., op. cit., pp. 224-226.

for sovereignty, then the matter would remain unresolved and Israeli troops would stay while the Palestinians continued to exercise his conception of self-rule.[8]

Trouble was brewing on the home front as well. The Israeli government announced October 25 its intention to expand existing Jewish settlements in reaction to U.S. intimations to West Bank leaders that Israel would eventually have to abandon them. Foreign Minister Dayan described a $15 million program to build 330 additional housing units to U.S. officials in Washington. The next day Begin declared that his government would continue to "implement its right to settle anywhere within the occupied West Bank and Gaza Strip." The decision nearly caused the recall of Egypt's negotiating delegation in Washington, forestalled only by a personal appeal by President Carter.[9]

In any case the peace treaty talks were suspended November 16 due to disagreements over the Egyptian demands for explicit linkage between the treaty and the autonomy plan and for a schedule detailing the stages of the autonomy plan's implementation, and over the Israeli demands that the peace treaty explicitly supersede all other Egyptian-Arab defense treaties and that ambassadors be exchanged during the first stages of the withdrawal from Sinai.[10]

In this atmosphere of stalemate and continued settlement activity, Peace Now decided to renew its activities. Its stated purpose was two-fold: to pressure the Begin government to stand "fully and whole-heartedly" behind the autonomy plan and to oppose the provocative actions of Gush Emunim and the government in the occupied territories.[11] Sure enough, at the end of December a band of Gush Emunim militants, aiming to test the government, set up two small encampments north of Jerusalem. Meanwhile, the military government announced that it would speed up seizure of West Bank land which it said it needed for military purposes. The intention was to complete the seizures before the autonomy plan was implemented. Though no indication was given of how much land would be taken, in the next few days some 3,100 dunams (about 625 acres) were

---

8. Ibid., p. 225.
9. Sobel, ed., op. cit., pp. 237-238; Haber, et. al., op. cit., p. 283.
10. Haber, et. al., op. cit., p. 291.
11. *Jerusalem Post*, December 6, 1978, and December 21, 1978.

expropriated from three villages.[12] In addition, religious militants in Hebron stirred up sectarian tensions by breaking into the Muslim prayer room in the Tomb of the Patriarchs, holy to both Muslims and Jews. The Israeli right was doing its utmost to try to undermine the peace process.

The turning point came at the beginning of January. Begin called on a group of Gush Emunim militants demonstrating near Nablus to end their action, promising "there will be settlement, there is no need for demonstrations. We have opened Samaria for settlement."[13] True to his word, he promised the Eilon Moreh core group (part of Gush Emunim) a site near Nablus. In response, some 3,000 Peace Now supporters rallied in Jerusalem.

With the support of 20 members of the Knesset, they attacked the Eilon Moreh decision. In a letter presented to Begin, the movement declared:

> "Your government will have to make up its mind; the peace process is in a crisis, not because of the formulation of this article or another in the suggested peace treaty. Basically, the crisis is one of confidence. Egypt does not believe that your government is sincere in its desire for peace with its neighbors, and suspects that your real goal is to keep control over the West Bank, and to be faithful to the goal of a greater Israel. The recent government decision reinforces these suspicions, and creates grave doubts, even among us, regarding the priorities of the Israeli government."[14]

Despite this protest, the Knesset Finance Committee approved a 709-million-pound budget for "thickening" settlements in all the occupied territories,[15] and the government announced that it planned to establish three new settlements in the Jordan river valley and at the southern end of the Gaza Strip.[16] In the meantime, public attention remained focused on the deadlocked peace negotiations. The U.S. had invited Israel's Foreign Minister Dayan and Egypt's Premier Mustafa Khalil back to Washington to

---

12. *Ha'aretz*, December 22, 1978; *Jerusalem Post*, December 14, 1978, December 18, 1978, and December 21, 1978.
13. *Ha'aretz*, January 5, 1979.
14. *Jerusalem Post*, January 14, 1979.
15. *Yediot Aharonot*, January 18, 1979.
16. Sobel, ed., op. cit., p. 244.

prepare the ground for a second round of Camp David talks. Three days earlier, on February 19, Peace Now, along with a group of M.K.'s representing the political spectrum from the left-wing Sheli to the National Religious Party, called on the government to show flexibility in the negotiations.[17]

For the most part, the movement was reduced to the role of a mere spectator during February and March, as Begin, Sadat, and Carter maneuvered behind the scenes and negotiated over the last sticking points of the hoped-for treaty. It did, however, organize in response to Gush Emunim's attacks on Carter during his visit to Israel in midMarch. As one spokesman for the movement said, "We mustn't allow the Israeli 'rejection front' to dominate the streets during the Carter visit."[18]

With the signing of the Egyptian-Israeli peace treaty in Washington on March 26, 1979, the process started by Sadat's visit to Jerusalem seemed irreversible. Two-thirds of the Sinai was to be returned to Egypt within nine months, and then Egypt and Israel were to exchange ambassadors. Israel was guaranteed freedom of passage through the Suez Canal, and Egypt would end its economic boycott of Israel—including selling Israel oil from the Sinai fields it had developed.[19]

But there was little rejoicing in Israel. Without the significant participation of Palestinian Arabs or Jordan, the negotiations on the plan for Palestinian self-rule in the West Bank and Gaza were doomed from the start. And the Begin government's stated positions and actions in the field did little to encourage their involvement, to say the least.

DEALING WITH "FACTS" ON THE GROUND

Moti Perry remembered the feeling within Peace Now then as worried. He said, "We saw these 'facts' on the West Bank—the Eilon Moreh decision, the expansion of Kiryat Arba [a Jewish suburb of Hebron]. It was clear they were doing it with government support."[20] At the time he was very pessimistic, saying that he was "100 percent convinced that the peace with

---

17. *Ma'ariv*, Februrary 20, 1979, *Jerusalem Post*, February 20, 1979.
18. *Jerusalem Post*, March 9, 1979.
19. Sobel, ed., op.cit., p. 253.
20. Interview with Moti Perry, January-February 1983.

Egypt will collapse unless Begin quickly changes course over the West Bank."[21] Evidence of Palestinian Arab dissatisfaction with the Camp David accords and the treaty was clear. Elias Freij, the mayor of Bethlehem and probably the most pro-American and moderate of the West Bank mayors, declared: "Peace cannot come to the Middle East because the Camp David agreements do not meet the minimum needs of the Palestinian people. What is that minimum? Recognition of the Palestinians' right of self-determination according to U.N. resolutions...What kind of autonomy is this that does not provide the basis for developing into a sovereign Palestinian state?"[22]

The battle for the West Bank began in earnest that spring. It was to be a mostly one-sided affair. The Israeli government, with its decisive majority in the Knesset, was essentially able to do as it pleased. The only weapon Peace Now had was its ability to mobilize and influence public opinion. At times the High Court of Israel played an important role in blocking or impeding government expropriations of land. The Labor Party ran a weak third in this struggle, partially because of its own internal problems and partially because of its interpretation of Israel's security needs on the West Bank. It remained a firm advocate of Israeli sovereignty and settlement in the so-called "security areas" of the Jordan Valley, the Gush Etzion bloc south of Jerusalem and in the Gaza Strip.[23]

Overpowered and limited by its own insistence on using democratic methods, Peace Now tended to focus its protests around concrete actions taken by the government or Gush Emunim, while at the same time trying to make symbolic and educational statements to the public about the dangers of the government's policy. As the year dragged on without any significant changes in Begin's and Sharon's attitude, Peace Now began to call for early elections and a change in governments. With time and experience, the movement started to sharpen its ideological position as well.

Peace Now opened its campaign with a beautifully symbolic action. At the end of April, some IDF reservists reported that they had seen residents of Kiryat Arba systematically using a power saw to uproot hundreds of

21. *Jerusalem Post*, July 27, 1979.
22. *Yediot Aharonot*, March 9, 1979.
23. *Davar*, December 8, 1978.

grape vines in a nearby Arab-owned vineyard.[24] Two men from Meir Kahane's fanatic fringe group Kach ("Thus") were arrested. Kach, an outgrowth of the Jewish Defense League, advocated the forcible expulsion of all of Israel's Arab population. After a delay of several days caused by their request for official permission to hold a demonstration at the vineyard on Ja'abari Hill in Hebron, Peace Now reacted by mobilizing two to three thousand supporters for a "peace planting" ceremony, replacing the vandalized vines.[25] Later, malicious rumors that the Arab villagers had uprooted the newly planted grape and olive trees turned out to be false. Indeed, Hebron Mayor Fahd Kawasmeh expressed his admiration for Peace Now's attempts to foster Jewish-Arab relations and attacked the intimation that West Bank Arabs could not tell the difference between peace-loving Jews and occupiers.[26]

The Peace Now leaflet distributed at the planting ceremony attacked the "chauvinist, extremist minority" for damaging the chances for peace and coexistence with the Palestinians by its vigilantism, land seizures, and vandalism. It called on the "silent majority" to "stand guard and nurture the budding peace with Egypt."[27] Oz Ve'Shalom, the religious dove group, condemned the destruction of the vines as a violation of the Jewish law (halacha) banning the destruction of growing fruit trees.[28] One participant at the demonstration, Shaul Markowitz, spoke to me later of the value of symbolic action: "I believe that someday we will have a peace agreement with these people and I want to show them that there is another Israel. Not just people who destroy, but also people who want a good relationship with the Palestinians. They were happy to see us...the people who were born under the gas and the occupation ... we have to do something to try to reduce the influence of what the government and Gush Emunim have done."[29]

Peace Now made its opposition clear in a four-part statement of principles that was based on the third concern of the Officers' Letter: rejection of

---

24. *Ha'aretz*, April 29, 1979.
25. *Jerusalem Post*, May 8, 1979; May 11, 1979; *Ha'aretz*, May 13, 1979.
26. *Jerusalem Post*, May 14, 1979, May 15, 1979.
27. *Israleft News Service*, no. 149, May 15, 1979, p.5.
28. *Jerusalem Post*, May 11, 1979.
29. Author interview with Shaul Markowitz, August 3, 1982.

rule over another people and maintenance of Israel's Jewish democratic character. The movement called on the government to view the autonomy plan as an interim arrangement towards a permanent solution of the Palestinian problem, to be willing to withdraw from the occupied territories "to borders negotiated according to security considerations alone," "to cease all settlement activities immediately," and to recognize "that without a solution to the Palestinian problem there can be no real peace," and therefore "the legitimate rights of the Palestinian people and their just demands must be taken into account."[30]

The Likud government showed no signs of heeding this advice. On April 22, the cabinet approved the creation of two new settlements on the West Bank—Eilon Moreh, south of Nablus, and Shiloh, once ostensibly only "an archeological dig." Said Begin, "there has never been an action more legal than settlement by Jews in all the territories of the land of Israel."[31] Earlier, at the beginning of March, it was revealed that the Ministry of Finance had approved a budget of 1.1 billion pounds for the support of 109 settlements and 12 outposts in the occupied territories— double that of the previous year. Some of this money was being used to make living on the West Bank financially attractive for young people who otherwise faced a worsening housing shortage in Israel. Several other settlements were in the advanced planning stages.

Gush Emunim responded to the peace treaty in a more extreme fashion, viewing the autonomy plan as satanic. First it threatened to lay the cornerstones for nine settlements the same day as the signing of the treaty. A month later, a group of women and children from Kiryat Arba illegally moved into the old Hadassah building in the heart of Hebron, drawing sharp criticism but no action from the government or the military administration.[32] But it was their secret, surprise establishment of the Eilon Moreh settlement in the beginning of June, after the Cabinet gave its final approval, that sparked a major confrontation between Peace Now, Gush Emunim and the Begin government.

Gush Emunim's action was clearly taken with the knowledge and

30. *Israleft News Service*, 149, May 15, 1979, p. 6.
31. Sobel, ed., op. cit. p. 270.
32. *Jerusalem Post*, June 19, 1979.

support of Ariel Sharon's Agriculture Ministry, if not the whole government. At eight in the morning of June 7, Arabs from a village near Nablus were served expropriation orders by the military government for land they owned on a hill in the area. Minutes later the settlement's founders arrived at the site. A rented helicopter brought in initial equipment, and three bull-dozers cleared a path up the hill. The army also helped by bringing large water tanks up the hill. The group's leader, Yossi Arziel, declared, "Here will arise the first Hebrew city in Samaria in 2000 years." Later that day Sharon himself visited the site. Criticism from the Labor opposition and other parties was swift, but no one knew just what Peace Now had planned.

Two days later, in a well-coordinated surprise action, the movement struck. Thousands of demonstrators blocked the path leading to the settle-ment with large boulders and posted guards to prevent anyone from enter-ing. They had prepared carefully for this action. "We knew they were planning to establish this settlement for several months," said Abu Vilan. The operation was planned in his office, he told me. It was "like a military force. When it happened, we just opened the papers, everyone went to his job, and two days later we brought a blockade to this settlement and we closed it for twenty-four hours." Some members of Peace Now were hesi-tant because the action was illegal. "Sure," responded Abu Vilan, "but the political issue was so strong we had to protest, and especially after they did it in an illegal way.[33]

Peace Now leaders attacked the settlement as "untimely and ill-conceived," considering the on-going autonomy talks with Egypt. More-over, Tzali Reshef pointed out, the government action was "illegal," saying that the owners had been issued the wrong writ, that they were not given fair warning to appeal the decision, and that the newly-bulldozed path ran through private fields not even covered by the expropriation order. He said that Peace Now would man the roadblock indefinitely and maintain "pas-sive resistance" up to the point of being physically removed by the authori-ties, stressing that they would not resort to violence.[34]

They demanded a meeting with Defense Minister Weizman, in part

---

33. Author interview with Abu Vilan, August 5, 1982.
34. *Jerusalem Post*, June 10, 1979.

because he himself had voted against the Eilon Moreh decision in June, and insisted that the issue be brought to the cabinet. After being threatened with eviction by the military commander of the region and staying overnight, they finally got their way. Weizman arrived the next morning and promised to bring their concerns to the cabinet.[35] Before the demonstrators left the site, M.K. Yossi Sarid, one of the movement's closest allies in the Knesset, declared to applause that "We are struggling to end the occupation...Will we always be able to restrain ourselves? Will we not reach a conclusion one day...that this government only understands threats, extortion and law-breaking?" Though Arab landowners appeared pleased with Peace Now's support, it was a frustrating conclusion for a bold action. Shortly after they left, bulldozers continued their interrupted work of tearing through a green cornfield to clear a path for a new road up to the settlement.[36]

The action generated a tremendous controversy, one that reverberated within Israel as well as abroad, and eventually reached the Israeli High Court. Zbigniew Brzezinski, for example, Carter's national security adviser, said that he was "very encouraged" by the Peace Now protest.[37] Begin intentionally refused to allow Weizman to raise the whole question in the cabinet as he had promised Peace Now, reacting sharply to the demonstration and comments from abroad. He reiterated Israel's "full right to settle in all parts of Eretz Yisrael," and berated critics who called the settlement a provocation, stating: "One recalls times when it was asserted that the very presence of Jews was of itself a 'provocation' ... If now there be Israelis of certain outlooks who accept the assumption that the presence of Jews alongside Arabs in our historic homeland, Eretz Yisrael, constitutes a 'provocation'—then shame on them. By doing so they adopt the evil path of the enemies of our people."[38]

This was not the first nor was it to be the last time that Begin would resort to the Jewish history of persecution in order to justify his actions and obliquely equate criticism with antisemitism. Rabbi Haim Druckman, head of the National Religious Party, accused Peace Now of cooperating with

---

35. *Ha'aretz*, June 10, 1979, and June 11, 1979.
36. *Jerusalem Post*, June 11, 1979.
37. Sobel, ed., op. cit., p. 271.
38. *Jerusalem Post*, June 12, 1979.

Israel's enemies, using phrases like "sabotage, incitement" and "helping the PLO."[39]

The debate in the Knesset a few days later was even stormier. Yossi Sarid argued that whatever the settlement did for Israel's security, its establishment seriously threatened Israel's national consensus—an even more important factor contributing to the nation's security. In response, Ariel Sharon lashed out at his detractors. First, he stated that "no 'fifth column' would halt the march of Zionism." He personally attacked Israeli T.V. reporter, Rafik Halabi, a Druze, for his report on the Eilon Moreh story that essentially made the same points on the settlement's illegality as did Peace Now. This remark unleashed a storm of insults directed at Sharon—"that's racism!", "you're simply inciting", "you're infantile, infantile." Sharon took it all in, smiling. "While you're heckling me here," he said, "we lay another meter of pipeline, another kilometer of road and build another house."

In another remark, he demeaned the whole spirit of the peace treaty, laying bare the government's true motives. Said Sharon, "the peace treaty was signed ... not because of Peace Now, but despite it; and not despite the settlements, but because of them."[40] Outside the debate, hundreds of Peace Now demonstrators and sympathizers continued to call for Eilon Moreh's dismantlement. The next day Begin repeated his election victory statement that, There will be more Eilon Morehs." He scoffed at the attacks on Sharon, saying "they will be forgotten in a generation's time, when every child will still learn about the military operations of Ariel Sharon."[41]

Continuing the protest a week later, some 40,000 people demonstrated outside the Tel Aviv Museum in support of Peace Now's call for the resignation of "that arrogant hallucinating" Menachem Begin and all his ministers and the dismantling of Eilon Moreh. It was the first big demonstration held by the movement since the eve of Camp David, and the turnout was impressive given the short time taken to organize it and the nature of the protest. People carried placards declaring that "Gush Emunim is strangling the state" and "occupation corrupts." One speaker stated that "Begin is the

39. Ibid.
40. *Jerusalem Post*, June 14, 1979.
41. *Jerusalem Post*, June 15, 1979.

subject of this demonstration. We are not protesting one Eilon Moreh, but the whole policy of occupation, eviction and coercion."[42]

Peace Now's original action received welcome support from an unexpected source—the Israeli High Court of Justice. All work on the Eilon Moreh settlement was halted pending resolution of a show cause order from the court stipulating that the state prove why construction should not be halted and the settlers not removed. The order was in response to a suit by seventeen Arab landowners whose land had been. seized by the army for the settlement and was based on earlier court decisions that had established that such actions had to be justified on grounds of national security.[43] Chief of Staff Rafael Eitan and Agriculture Minister Ariel Sharon provided statements to the court arguing the security value of the settlement, while Defense Minister Weizman, Deputy Prime Minister Yadin, Foreign Minister Dayan, former Chief of Staff M.K. Haim Bar-Lev and former IDF chief of operations Matti Peled gave affidavits arguing the opposite.[44]

Four months later the court handed down its decision: Eilon Moreh must go. In their statements, the judges criticized both the secretive manner of the settlement's establishment, and its dubious security value. According to the Geneva Convention, expropriation of conquered lands is permissible only for security reasons. On this point they were inclined to accept the deposition of Bar-Lev: that the settlement's specific location, near a large military camp, provided no additional strategic value; and because it was located close to an area densely populated by Arabs it might be a security liability.[45]

More importantly, they attacked the obvious political motivations involved in the original Eilon Moreh decision. Justice M. Landau wrote: "We have had enough indications from the evidence before us that both the Ministerial committee and the Cabinet majority were decisively influenced by reasons lying in a Zionist world-view of the settlement of the Whole Land of Israel. Would the decision of the political level to establish

42. *Jerusalem Post*, June 17, 1979, *Ha'aretz*, June 17, 1979.
43. *Jerusalem Post*, June 21, 1979.
44. *Jerusalem Post*, June 21, 1979, *Ha'aretz*, June 19, 1979, July 4, 1979.
45. Justice Vitkon's statement, in *Israleft News Service*, No.157, November 1, 1979, p. 7, *Ha'aretz*, November 1979.

the settlement at that site have been taken had it not been for the pressure of Gush Emunim and the political-ideological reasons which were before the political level? I have been convinced that had it not been for these reasons, the decision would not have been taken in the circumstances which prevailed at the time."[46]

The court ordered Eilon Moreh evacuated by November 22. It was a significant victory for Peace Now and the opposition, but it was to prove to be a hollow one.

---

46. Justice M. Landau's statement, in *Israleft News Service*, No. 157, November 1, 1979, p. 6- 7.

CHAPTER 4
"SANE ZIONISM" VS "GREATER ISRAEL"

AS PEACE NOW leader Abu Vilan saw it, the Eilon Moreh incident gave impetus to a national debate on the question: "What kind of state will Israel be—a bi-national state or a Jewish democratic one?"[1] All that summer and into the fall, seminars and forums were held under the movement's sponsorship. At one held in Tel Aviv in late July, former prime minister Yitzhak Rabin of the Labor Party told a packed house that to make peace "there is no alternative but to hand back some territory ... The state of Israel will not survive if it must include some 1.7 million Arab citizens, and a Jewish state will not survive if those Arabs' civil rights are abrogated.[2] His was just a moderate statement of the problem. Attitudes within Peace Now ranged from those who favored a territorial compromise along the lines of the Allon plan to those who spoke of a Palestinian state as inevitable.[3] But there was general agreement that such a discussion was secondary to the necessity to oppose the negative and provocative actions of the government and Gush Emunim.

Controversy surrounding Jewish-Arab relations on the West Bank arose again at the end of the summer. For the first time, Deputy Prime Minister

---

1. Author interview with Abu Vilan, August 5, 1982.
2. *Jerusalem Post*, July 25, 2979.
3. *Jerusalem Post*, July 27, 1979, *Ha'aretz*, March 11, 1983.

Yadin asserted himself against Ariel Sharon. At the end of August, the Ministerial Defense Committee had decided to "enlarge" four settlements in Samaria. Yadin had been abroad and missed the meeting. When he returned, he discovered that Sharon was actually working on setting up four new settlements. Yadin asked, "How can you talk about enlarging existing settlements if they are 19 to 20 kilometers from the original ones?" Weizman and even Begin were surprised at Sharon's duplicity. As the knowledge of Sharon's latest plot spread, dissension within the Democratic Movement for Change grew with some central figures calling for a decision on the party's continuing participation in the coalition.[4] In support, some 300 Peace Now members held a protest vigil outside of Sharon's office in Jerusalem attacking his plans to seize Arab-owned lands in densely populated portions of the West Bank as provocative and wasteful of scarce national funds.[5]

A new move by Gush Emunim in Hebron then shifted the movement's attention. Since the signing of the peace treaty, forty women and children had illegally squatted in the former Hadassah building in the heart of Hebron. Despite Begin's opposition—"No one will dictate to the government how, where, and when to settle," he said—no action had been taken to remove them. Indeed, in June, Sharon had visited the group, praising their "stubbornness and perseverance", and seeing to it that restrictions on their movement be lifted.[6] Then, in the middle of September, Gush Emunim announced its intention to occupy seven new flats there, which had been renovated at government expense. In response, between twenty and thirty religious members of Peace Now attempted to enter Hebron to demonstrate against Gush Emunim, but were prevented from doing so by an army roadblock.[7]

The next day the Israeli cabinet abrogated a 1967 law prohibiting Israelis from buying Arab-owned land in the occupied territories. The intent of the law had been to centralize authority on Jewish settlement in the government's hands. Jewish settlers had pushed for the change, claiming that the need to confiscate land would be reduced if land

---

4. *Ha'aretz*, September 3, 1979; September 11, 1979; *Yediot Aharonot*, September 3, 1979.
5. *Jerusalem Post*, September 14, 1979.
6. *Ha'aretz*, June 28, 1979.
7. *Jerusalem Post*, September 18, 1979.

purchase was allowed. This time some twenty-five academics and physicians representing Peace Now did manage to get into Hebron to hold a short demonstration by the Hadassah building.

The following day several hundred Peace Now supporters tried to enter Hebron, but they were again stopped by a roadblock. Complaining that Gush Emunim had never been refused permission to demonstrate on the West Bank, they sat and blocked the Jerusalem-Hebron road for three hours.[8] Some frustrated Jewish settlers who were stopped on their way home started fistfights with them. On the other hand, the protest generated some good will. One Palestinian Arab, Muhammed Hasan Shenuar, told a reporter that "I am glad there are demonstrations like these. I would prefer to be delayed twenty hours rather than see the military government expropriate twenty dunams."[9]

These small demonstrations were relatively ineffective, except for their symbolic and educational value and the media attention they got. As it was, the decision to demonstrate illegally on the West Bank had been a difficult one for the movement. Dedi Zucker later told me that "The arguments were like hell ... because it was illegal, because it was 'radicalization'." People wondered "how will the Arabs accept us" and feared being seen as "Arab lovers fighting for their interests, not our interests."[10] Many Peace Now leaders remarked that this was the beginning of a frustrating time for them. Public attention was focused elsewhere—on the economy, the Sinai withdrawal, or government scandals.

At the time of the demonstrations in Hebron, for example, the press headlines were filled with revelations about the "Pinto" affair. An Israeli lieutenant, Daniel Pinto, had tortured and strangled to death four Lebanese farm workers during the short-lived Israeli invasion of southern Lebanon in 1978. He had been sentenced first to twelve years imprisonment, then eight years, and then Chief of Staff Eytan reduced the punishment to only two years in jail (for first degree murder). It was not the first case of such leniency.[11] In the atmosphere of recriminations and denials that followed, Peace Now's concerns were pushed to the back burner.

---

8. *Jerusalem Post*, September 20, 1979.
9. *Ha'aretz*, September 19, 1979. A dunam is 1,000 square meters, or roughly a quarter-acre.
10. Author interview with Dedi Zucker, August 18, 1982.
11. *Al-Hamishmar*, September 16, 1979.

Public opinion polls however continued to show popular support for Peace Now's positions at the time. A survey done by the PORY Institute for the newspaper *Ha'aretz* showed that 72.4% of the respondents felt "there could be no peace agreement with all the Arab states without the resolution of the Palestinian question." This figure showed a slight rise since December of 1978, when 69.3% agreed with the statement. On the negative side 37.3% believed there could be no peace between Israel and the Arab states. Another positive sign was that a growing number of Israelis believed the government should open negotiations with the PLO once it recognized Israel's right to exist. This percentage increased from 16.4% in May to 28.6% in September.[12]

Pressure on the Cabinet from the right built during early October. Gush Emunim demanded 200,000 dunams for Jewish settlement on the West Bank.[13] Threatening to draw support away from Begin on the right, the ultra-nationalist Tehiya party was formed on October 8—calling for annexation of the occupied territories and retention by Israel of the settlements in Northern Sinai.[14] Led by renegade Likudnik Geula Cohen and Professor Yuval Ne'eman, the Tehiya party was to prove to be a major thorn in the government's side (a pattern we see again in current times with far-right minister Itamar Ben-Gvir and Bezalel Smotrich exerting similar leverage on the ruling Likud coalition of Benjamin Netanyahu). Predictably, the Israeli Cabinet voted unanimously, on October 14, to expand seven existing settlements in the West Bank using about 40,000 dunams of state land. Supposedly the threatened resignation of Moshe Dayan prevented the ministers from approving the seizure of privately-owned Arab land.[15]

In response to the Cabinet's recent series of decisions, Peace Now organized a massive demonstration "for sane Zionism" in Tel Aviv with the declared support of twenty M.K.'s. Some 80,000 protestors marched in the rain carrying signs reading "Expanding settlements will continue the wars," "Begin go home," and "Gush Emunim is Israel's fascist movement." Speakers took a strident tone. "We have sufficient numbers to stop the government and tell it: You have gone far enough," shouted Abu Vilan.

12. *Ha'aretz*, December 24, 1978; September 25, 1979, *Jerusalem Post*, September 28, 1979.
13. *Jerusalem Post*, October 15, 1979.
14. *Yediot Aharonot*, October 9, 1979.
15. Sobel, ed. , op. cit. , p. 273.

"We are here: Thou shalt not pass." Echoing one placard that said, "Raise the Palmach," a reference to the Labor movement's pre-1948 militia, Abu Vilan called for "the creation of a new force, Zionist and Democratic, that will work and fight."[16] The movement's frustration with seemingly ineffective forms of protest in the face of the Begin-Sharon steamroller was beginning to show.

The choice of the slogan "Sane Zionism" was no accident. In the preceding months, the Peace Now movement had begun to define, through internal discussions in its many branches, its relation to the Palestinian question. Thus, at this large demonstration in Tel Aviv it called on the government of Israel "to take the initiative in breaking the cycle of Israeli-Palestinian hostility." Cognizant of the centrality of the Palestinians to any comprehensive peace settlement, Peace Now called for "negotiations with any Palestinian body which accepts the path of negotiation as the only means of solving the Middle Eastern conflict" in accordance with the following principles:

- The Palestinians will recognize Israel's right to exist as a sovereign Jewish state within secure borders and will abandon the use of terror. For its part, Israel will recognize the right of the Palestinians to a national entity. The fulfillment of this right must not endanger Israel's security.
- Both sides will conduct the negotiations in the firm belief that only through mutual compromise of political demands, based on the historical rights of both peoples, can peace be brought to the area.
- Israel will relinquish its basic claim to sovereignty over the West Bank and the Gaza Strip and will be guided in its demands by security considerations alone. During the negotiations all settlement activities and legislative proceedings which impede the peace process will cease.
- The Palestinian representatives will be accorded status equal to that of the representatives of all states participating in the

---

16. *Ha'aretz*, October 21, 1979, *Jerusalem Post*, October 21, 1979.

resolution of the Palestinian problem and the problem of the West Bank and the Gaza Strip.

- The autonomy proposed in the Camp David accords constitutes a transitional stage on the way to a comprehensive settlement of the Arab-Israeli conflict. This autonomy plan is linked to the construction of peace with Egypt and should be implemented in the areas of the West Bank and Gaza.

- The negotiations between the parties participating in the peace process will be conducted on the basis of the Camp David accords and Security Council resolution 242. Israel will view the Palestinian issue as that of a people possessing national rights, and not as a refugee problem alone.[17]

Such a formulation of a solution to the Israeli-Palestinian conflict was not in itself new or original. Leftists and doves had propounded similar conceptions for many years, with little popular success. Indeed, the original Movement for Another Zionism had also spoken of the Palestinian problem as a problem of conflicting nationalisms and historical rights to the land. As Dedi Zucker admitted to me later, "We never created a new ideology. Sane Zionism is a phrase that was used before. The success was that we mobilized people behind these slogans in a non-parliamentary way.[18]

Peace Now embarked on this declaration of principles for Israeli-Palestinian negotiations partially in preparation for an upcoming Israeli-Palestinian conference that was to take place in Washington. The movement sought to clarify its own stand on contacts with PLO members by drafting the declaration. In the end it decided to allow six representatives to attend the conference on the condition that no members of PLO institutions participate.[19] Such a stand was taken to protect the movement's credibility among the Israeli public which nearly unanimously viewed contacts with the PLO as treasonous.

Yet, according to Moti Perry, Peace Now had several times had indirect

---

17. Peace Now pamphlet, October 1979.
18. Author interview with Dedi Zucker, August 18, 1982.
19. *Ha'aretz*, September 2, 1979.

contact with PLO supporters and members, starting as early as sometime in 1979. The purpose of these contacts was to strengthen the Israeli peace camp and cause a moderation in PLO official policy. Perry said that Peace Now—using journalists, people in Europe and Palestinians in the U.S. as intermediaries—had expressed its willingness to make a joint statement with the PLO calling for a Palestinian state on the West Bank and the Gaza Strip and peace with Israel within the Green Line, based on the above principles. Supposedly, Arafat's circle of key advisers was interested, but feared a bloodbath in the PLO. In addition, he noted, "They say Peace Now is not the government; their gain would only be the strengthening of the Israeli peace forces." His response: "Peace Now is the only hope they have."[20]

After their demonstration of 80,000 people in Tel Aviv, Peace Now's activists were tired, but their spirits were temporarily raised by the High Court of Justice's decision ordering the dismantling of Eilon Moreh (discussed above). Though the deadline for the settlement's evacuation was set for November 22, the Begin government was dragging its feet. Mattityahu Drobles, co-chairman of the World Zionist Organization's Settlement Department, complained that the court's judgement would cause the waste of 30 million Israeli pounds already invested in Eilon Moreh.[21] In a compromise move of questionable legal validity, 125 dunams of land belonging to the neighboring village was returned, while the government gave itself a six-week extension in which to negotiate with the settlers, offering them another site called Jabal Kabir. The November 22 deadline passed. Twenty-one Arab villagers whose land was still occupied by the settlers then appealed again to the court, demanding that the army remove all the settlers immediately.[22]

While the government stalled, Peace Now again prepared to take to the streets. At first it kept its plans unclear, partially to keep the authorities off balance and partially because the leadership itself was divided on whether to stage massive demonstrations in the cities or to protest at Eilon Moreh itself. Rumors spread that the movement would evict the settlers themselves, but Omri Padan, a central leader in Jerusalem, squelched them,

---

20. Author interview with Moti Perry, January-February 1983.
21. *Yediot Aharonot Weekly*, November 16, 1979.
22. *Jerusalem Post*, November 25, 1979, *Davar*, November 18, 1979.

saying that that would be "out of the question. It would only result in violence and we are not going to do the government's work for it."[23]

In the end, they decided to march on the Prime Minister's residence, protesting the government's settlements and economic policy. Forming a torch-lit circle, they buried a coffin in its center with the statements "Here lies buried the peace agreement" and "Here lies buried 150 million pounds" written on it. The use of the slogan "Stop Settlements, Funds to the Slums," linking the two issues, was a relatively new one for Peace Now. It did have the effect of attracting several dozen supporters of the radical "Black Panthers" protest group, which had helped orchestrate violent protests against recent price hikes. After threatening to violently disrupt the rally, one of their leaders, Sa'adia Marciano, was allowed to address the 5,000-strong crowd.[24]

Several hundred of the Peace Now demonstrators then slept outside the Prime Minister's office in order to greet the cabinet members on their way to and from the weekly cabinet meeting. The cabinet did not address the issue of the settlements in that meeting, nor was it disturbed by the protesters' chants. "Thank goodness the cabinet room is well insulated," said cabinet secretary Aryeh Naor after the meeting. A young woman heard this remark and shouted back, "Yes, insulated in mind, spirit, and heart."[25]

The settlers at Eilon Moreh eventually did accept the government's offer to move them to Jabal Kabir as soon as the site was ready. Seventy million pounds were appropriated for that purpose.[26] Meanwhile, at the suggestion of three members of Begin's Herut party, the government began to consider ways to redefine the legal status of the West Bank so that it would no longer be considered occupied and settlement could take place for other than solely security reasons.[27] This possibility was welcomed by Gush Emunim.

The January 3 deadline that the Cabinet had set for itself approached and the new site was not ready because of bad weather. So they decided

---

23. *Jerusalem Post*, November 16, 1979, November 19, 1979.
24. *Jerusalem Post*, November 25, 1979, *Ha'aretz*, November 25, 1979.
25. *Jerusalem Post*, November 26, 1979.
26. *Davar*, December 21, 1979.
27. *Ha'aretz*, November 23, 1979, *Jerusalem Post*, December 12, 1979.

that they were not in any rush and left no new deadline for carrying out the High Court's order.[28] Evidence later surfaced that the government and the settlers colluded to secretly buy some land adjoining the Eilon Moreh site from unsuspecting landowners in the area. After the High Court's decision, Ariel Sharon had convinced Begin of Eilon Moreh's symbolic importance, and with his permission had okayed the transfer of some ten million pounds to Gush Emunim to acquire 100 dunams at greatly inflated prices.[29]

Peace Now had decided beforehand they would continue their protest against the illegal Eilon Moreh settlement. Thus they were well prepared to respond to the cabinet's latest decision postponing the removal of Eilon Moreh. Braving a torrential downpour and icy winds, some three hundred activists blocked the entrance to the settlement, forcing a meeting with Weizman and by coincidence trapping Ariel Sharon inside the settlement for five hours.

"We left early Saturday morning from Kibbutz Negba with two big trucks filled with some very large blocks," remembered Abu Vilan, who had also helped plan the first Eilon Moreh action. "A small car was sent forward to see exactly what there was, and we saw that Mr. Sharon was going on a tour, and so we went back to bring the blocks. And it was a race, who will come first. A half a minute before he came back to the entrance, we brought the blocks."[30] Soldiers stopped them from unloading the blocks, but then Peace Now members chained themselves to the trucks, forming a human blockade and demanding to see Weizman. At first, he refused to discuss anything with them before the road was cleared, but then acceded to their demand to bring two concerns to the cabinet: that the scheduled cabinet discussion of a change in the legal status of the West Bank settlements be removed from the agenda and that a moratorium on new settlements be imposed as long as the autonomy negotiations continued.[31]

Though movement leaders expressed their satisfaction (and glee at

---

28. *Ha'aretz*, December 31, 1979.

29. *Davar*, January 15, 1979, *Ha'aretz*, January 1, 1980, *Ma'ariv*, January 31, 1980, February 7, 1980.

30. Author interview with Abu Vilan, August 5, 1982.

31. *Jerusalem Post*, January 6, 1980, *Yediot Aharonot*, January 6, 1980.

having caught Sharon in the rain and mud) with the whole Eilon Moreh series of protests, they knew that they had fought a losing battle. The Eilon Moreh settlers were eventually moved to another site on February 3, and no change in government policy occurred. Speaking with me a few years later, Abu Vilan expressed the feeling within the movement: "Until the Camp David agreement, I think we had an influence. In the struggle over the new settlements they won, because they established them and we didn't succeed in stopping them. As Arik Sharon said, 'the dogs shout, but the convoy passes ...' From that time we felt that, after a year's struggle without big results, the only thing we can do politically is to try to change this government."[32]

The second Eilon Moreh episode marked a definite turning point in the movement's strategy. Yet before it could concentrate its attentions on the goal of helping to bring down the Begin government, it was forced to confront a tidal wave of official and press criticism of its activities abroad and, by implication, of its political legitimacy in Israel.

PEACE NOW AND DIASPORA JEWRY

From its very beginning, Peace Now was involved in political activity abroad. Its contacts with Jews from the diaspora and its role in presenting a critical view of Israeli policy were the source of all the controversy. The issue was particularly important in relation to American Jewry, who then and still now clearly have a disproportionate amount of influence on U.S policy toward the region.

For many years after World War II, the American Jewish community attempted to maintain a unified pro-Israel stand towards questions of U.S.-Israel relations. Suppression of dissent was justified by arguing that on questions of Israel's security, Jews not living in Israel should defer judgment to elected Israeli governments. Supposedly criticism only aided Israel's enemies. But after the 1967 war when Israel suddenly seemed to be in a more secure position, dissenting positions began to surface more frequently. In the early 1970's, an American Jewish group called Breira ("Alternative") attempted to provide an outlet for such opinions, but its

---

32. Author interview with Abu Vilan, August 5, 1982.

leadership was effectively blacklisted and red-baited by the more main-stream Jewish establishment, forcing Breira to disband after only four years of existence. Such dissent could not be long contained, however. With Begin's election, larger numbers of American Jews began to express dissatisfaction with the direction Israel was taking. It was natural that these Jews would come to identify with and support Peace Now.

The initial contacts between Peace Now and diaspora Jews were initiated by the latter, in the form of letters and visits. Telegrams or advertisements of support, like the early declaration from thirty-seven prominent American Jews noted earlier, were totally unsolicited.[33] In the fall of 1979, a delegation of six Peace Now representatives set off for the U.S. at the invitation of American Jewish groups. It was after this tour that the whole debate started.

In a series of articles in the *Jerusalem Post* at the end of December, Shmuel Katz, former information adviser to the Prime Minister and a leader of the opposition to the treaty with Egypt, took Peace Now to task. First, he attacked it for accepting support and funds from, among others, former members of Breira (which he characterized as a pro-PLO organization), suggesting its guilt by association with "known anti-Zionists." He referred to the public appearances made in the U.S. by Shulamit Koenig, an early Israeli supporter of Peace Now, and argued that her support for the PLO as "freedom fighters," and for U.S. pressure on Israel, and her encouragement of the ending of American Jewry's monetary support for Israel, represented "the authentic voice of Peace Now." Lastly, he suggested that Peace Now's criticism, intentionally or unintentionally, aided the "worldwide coalition of forces engaged in trying to achieve the reduction of Israel."[34]

These criticisms were essentially repeated in harsher terms by Israel's Ambassador to France, Meir Rosenne, when a Peace Now delegation toured western Europe in January. He called on local Jewish organizations and journalists not to help publicize the group's visit, which he termed "a blow against the security and interests of Israel" and "an insult to the

---

33. *Ha'aretz*, February 15, 1980, *Jerusalem Post*, December 28, 1979.
34. *Jerusalem Post*, December 21, 1979; December 14, 1979; January 14, 1980.

memory of Israel's heroes and martyrs."[35] Likud Member of Knesset Avraham Sharir went even further, accusing Peace Now of "subversive activities" and suggesting the prosecution of two of its leaders who had toured the U.S.[36] Were these various accusations part of an orchestrated campaign to discredit the Peace Now movement? There is some evidence supporting this possibility. Whatever the case, they clearly represented a threat to the movement's legitimacy in Israel.

The movement fought back valiantly. It disavowed any official connection with Shulamit Koenig and vehemently denied having participated on any platforms with PLO representatives or having received financial support from PLO supporters. Moving to the more substantial criticisms of their activity, movement spokesmen argued that their work was actually helping to retain for Israel the loyalty and support of Jews who were otherwise becoming very alienated by the Begin government. One proffered example of this alienation was the statement by Ted Mann, head of the Conference of Presidents of Major American Jewish Organizations, who said that he believed 90 to 95% of North American Jewry opposed the government's policies in the occupied territories.

Regarding their right to voice dissent abroad, Peace Now's leaders noted that for years members of all of Israel's political parties had made public appearances abroad. More recently, according to Mordecai Bar-On, former IDF chief education officer and an older Peace Now activist, "The Jewish agency sent Hanan Porat and other Gush Emunim leaders abroad to present their case to Jews outside Israel."[37] They also supported the right of Jews abroad to hear more than one interpretation of developments in Israel, as part of what Zionists consider to be the organic link between Israel and world Jewry. Moreover, they argued that an influential community like American Jewry was already a factor in Israeli politics. As Omri Padan pointed out, "When Begin returns from the U.S. and announces that all of American Jewry is behind him, he already pulls them, intentionally or not, into the public discussion in Israel."[38]

Peace Now's loyalty to Israel was never seriously in question, at least if

---

35. *Ha'aretz*, January 24, 1980.
36. *Jerusalem Post*, January 27, 1980.
37. *Jerusalem Post*, January 29, 1980, *Hotam*, January 18, 1980.
38. *Ha'aretz*, February 15, 1980.

one can judge by the support it received in newspaper editorials and from political leaders. Nor was its right to dissent. But it remained most vulnerable to the accusation that it was playing with fire by bringing its message abroad. As one critic wrote: "The fact that they cannot be responsible for the motivations of all those who have jumped on their bandwagon and claim to speak in their name, and that they cannot guarantee what use and misuse will be made of the criticism they do voice abroad, should make them doubly careful."[39]

The charge that carried the most weight was that Peace Now was hurting Israel's position by giving fuel to critics and enemies of the state. One response to this attack was that enemies of Israel would find arguments against it without need of Peace Now or any group. But their strongest defense was to point out that it was more likely that it was the Begin government's ideological intransigence that was hurting Israel's international image and support. Dr. Leon Sheleff of Tel Aviv University, writing in the *Jerusalem Post*, pinpointed this weakness in the arguments of Peace Now critics by noting that Shmuel Katz had accused them of "trying to achieve the reduction of Israel." "Which Israel?" asked Sheleff. Greater Israel or the State of Israel as recognized by the international community (i.e. pre-1967 borders)? He added, "On this crucial issue—willingness to countenance a partition of Eretz Yisrael for the sake of peace—it is the Herut ideologists who are—and have always been—in the minority. The Peace Now movement came into being and continues to exist in order to remind Begin and his supporters, present and erstwhile, of this simple fact, so difficult for them to accept. In this respect, Peace Now speaks with the authentic voice of the majority of Israel."[40]

By representing the half of Israel that did not support Menachem Begin, Peace Now was arguably helping to strengthen Israel's image in the eyes of the world. Why then the criticism from the Israeli right-wing? One can conclude that it was due to their justified fear that by forcefully articulating a Zionist alternative to the Greater Israel school of thought, Peace Now strengthened Jewish dissent in the diaspora as well as in Israel and contributed to the delegitimizing of the Begin government. It is a measure

---

39. *Jerusalem Post*, February 1, 1980.
40. *Jerusalem Post*, December 28, 1979, *Ha'aretz*, February 15, 1980.

of the movement's power that it warranted such attention. As long as he was in office, Prime Minister Begin almost always referred to Peace Now when he attacked his critics—seeing them as a major source of opposition.

"ELECTIONS NOW"

Events began to overshadow the polemics again at the end of January, leading to the deaths and maiming of both Jews and Arabs on the West Bank. On January 21 a yeshiva student from Kiryat Arba was shot and killed while he was shopping in the Hebron Casbah. A Syrian-supported faction of the PLO took responsibility for the action.[41] It followed a period of heightened Jewish-Arab tension in Hebron, during which 600 dunams of Arab land north of Kiryat Arba were fenced off and effectively taken for the expansion of the settlement. Gush Emunim settlers also continued to squat in the Hadassah building and attempted to assert the precedence of Jewish religious rights over Muslim rights at the Tomb of the Patriarchs (also the Ibrahimi Mosque).[42] Following the murder a curfew was imposed on the town. Jewish settlers roamed the streets "asserting" their precedence, as one put it. Kiryat Arba residents demanded that large areas be taken over for the expansion of their settlement, as well as all the areas in the old city of Hebron where Jews had lived in the past.[43]

Begin was in accord with this idea and announced that the cabinet would soon take up the issue.[44] Ariel Sharon proposed that the government populate five buildings in the town with Jews, as a "Zionist answer" to the murder of the yeshiva student.[45] Hebron's Mayor Fahd Kawasmeh responded, "If they would like to return, we won't refuse. But we ask to be allowed to return to our houses in Lod, Jaffa, Ramle, and Jerusalem."[46]

On February 10 the cabinet approved in principle the right of Jews to resettle in the heart of Hebron.[47] But widespread opposition caused Begin

---

41. *Ha'aretz*, February 1, 1980, *Yediot Aharonot*, February 1, 1980.
42. *Jerusalem Post*, January 3, 1980, January 28, 1980.
43. *Davar*, February 3, 1980, *Jerusalem Post*, February 3, 1980, *Ha'aretz*, February 4, 1980.
44. *Yediot Aharanot*, February 4, 1980.
45. *Ha'aretz*, February 4, 1980.
46. *Jerusalem Post*, February 5, 1980.
47. *The New York Times*, February 11, 1980.

to move slowly in executing this decision. The U.S. State Department, for example, responded with a strong understatement, saying that the cabinet's decision could be "a step backwards in the peace process and could well have serious consequences," noting that it raised "a basic question of Israel's commitment to full autonomy."[48] Several of the Liberal Party and D.M.C. ministers in the cabinet were also known to have strong reservations to the idea.[49] Peace Now held vigils outside the government offices while the cabinet deliberated.

The day before the government decision was to be made, Peace Now held demonstrations in Israel's three major cities, drawing some ten thousand people. According to a poll done for the *Jerusalem Post* by the Modi'in Ezrahi Applied Research Center in the middle of March, 51.4% of the Israeli public opposed Jewish settlement in Hebron, while 46.3% favored it.[50] Another poll by the PORY institute, commissioned by *Ha'aretz*, found that to the specific question, "are you for or against the settling of Jews in the buildings in Hebron," 52.2% answered negatively while 35.8% answered in the affirmative.[51]

In this atmosphere of worldwide and domestic opposition, especially vocal Palestinian opposition, the decision to settle in Hebron seemed to become almost a matter of national honor for Begin and Sharon. Mayor Kawasmeh was prevented from traveling to New York to address the U.N. Security Council on the topic. Gush Emunim kept up its calls for settlement and continued to "assert" their presence in the city through acts of vandalism and violence. On March 23, the government took the plunge, deciding "to work towards the development of the Jewish complex in the Jewish Quarter of Hebron, with the objective of reviving it," by establishing a Yeshiva and a field school in the old city and by adding a third floor to the Hadassah building. The cabinet vote was eight to six with three abstentions.[52]

Gush Emunim was overjoyed, while Hebron city leaders called the decision the "crowning achievement in a policy of repression on the West

---

48. Sobel, ed. op. cit., p. 273.
49. *Jerusalem Post*, March 16, 1980.
50. *Jerusalem Post*, March 24, 1980, March 16, 1980.
51. *Ha'aretz*, March 16, 1980.
52. Israel Government Press Office, March 23, 1980, March 24, 1980.

Bank." Other Palestinian mayors joined them in condemning the decision. Said Mohammed Milhem, mayor of nearby Halhul, "We have now started losing hope in all possibilities for the peace process. What has been taken by force can never be regained, except by force."[53] Yet again, steps taken by the Begin government reinforced the radicalization of West Bank inhabitants, undermining the chances for a peaceful solution.

Peace Now effectively changed its name to "Elections Now" when it took to the nation's highways to protest the settlement in Hebron. Some 25,000 people covered the main road from Haifa through Tel Aviv to Jerusalem calling for Begin to resign. A leaflet distributed by the demonstrators stated, "The settlement in Hebron encompasses all the erroneous priorities of the government and proves that this government has learned nothing. The public must recognize that this government has reached the end of its road, and the Israeli public—if it knows how to fight for its security and well-being—can bring this government down."[54] In addition, several busloads of Jerusalem slum residents belonging to the Ohelim self-help organization participated in the demonstration, showing that Peace Now's recent emphasis on the economic drain that settlements placed on Israel's resources for social spending would perhaps attract the Sephardi poor to the predominantly Ashkenazi, middle-class movement. "Money to the slums, not to the settlements" became a new movement slogan.

From this point on, Peace Now focused its activity on bringing down the government. This was despite the traumatic series of events that unfolded in Hebron at the beginning of May. On their way home to Kiryat Arba from prayers in Hebron, five Jewish settlers were killed and sixteen wounded in a terrorist attack. The Israeli authorities reacted swiftly, demolishing houses near the Hadassah building and deporting Hebron's Mayor Fahd Kawasmeh, Halhul's Mohammed Milhem, and the Islamic judge (qadi) of Hebron. Both mayors, supporters of a Palestinian state, were also on the record as favoring co-existence with the state of Israel.[55]

Defense Minister Weizman justified the retaliation against the mayors by claiming that it was their verbal incitement that led others to the

---

53. *Jerusalem Post*, March 24, 1980, March 25, 1980.
54. lsraleft News Service, No. 167, April 15, 1980, pp. 4-5.
55. Halabi, op. cit., p.163.

terrorist attack. No mention was made, of course, of the several recent acts of organized vandalism by Gush Emunim settlers in the area, or of the deliberate destruction of supposedly illegal crops in the Mount Hebron area by Israeli crop-dusters spraying poison.[56] Palestinians on the West Bank responded with several days of strikes, protests and stoning of army vehicles. Critics of the government in the Knesset and the press attacked Begin for not having evacuated the original squatters in the Hadassah building over a year ago. Peace Now preferred to concentrate on the underlying issue: the Begin government.

Characteristically, the movement turned to the two traditional means of influence at its disposal—the press and the streets. Every Sunday's cabinet meeting was greeted by a protest vigil. On May 20, Peace Now published an ad declaring "Our way is not their's." The ad attacked "extremists in the public and within the government" for endangering Israel's future and called for "peace and security through compromise and partition," "coexistence and tolerance." It was signed by nineteen M.K.s and an impressive list of religious leaders, former generals, academics, industrialists, and artists.

On Peace Now's central concern, the willingness to exchange territories for peace, 68% of the continued to support territorial compromise on the West Bank. Only 11.5% supported full annexation. Even among Likud voters, that is, supporters of Begin, only 39.6% favored annexation or the continuation of the status quo.[57] Key opposition figures began to take up Peace Now's demand. By the time Ezer Weizman resigned from the government in late May, after having gradually been isolated for his more moderate or at least pragmatic views, the entire political opposition was calling for Begin's resignation.

Before the next series of Peace Now anti-government demonstrations, the situation on the West Bank took another turn for the worse. Settlers began forming "regional security committees" to insure their "adequate" protection. Fears of the development of an armed Jewish underground were given more stimulus when authorities discovered a large arms cache in a Jerusalem yeshiva. Rabbi Meir Kahane and an aide were apprehended

---

56. *Israleft News Service*, No. 168, May 1, 1980, p.6, *Davar*, April 15, 1980.
57. Peace Now pamphlet, June 1980.

and held under administrative detention, a punishment used until then only against Arabs, in suspicion of their being involved in this development. Evidence later surfaced showing that the arms were intended to be used to blow up the al-Aqsa Mosque in the Old City of Jerusalem.[58]

Peace Now called on the government to prevent Gush Emunim from establishing a "private army," fearing clashes between them and the IDF that might lead to a civil war. Instead, Chief of Staff Eitan ordered that all settlers be posted to the regional defense units of the occupation army and be given responsibility for policing and patrol missions in West Bank towns.[59] Even if it was to be ousted soon, the Begin government was laying mines that the next government would find difficult to dismantle harmlessly.

The June 2 maiming of Ramallah Mayor Karim Khalaf and Nablus Mayor Bassam Shak'a and unsuccessful attempt on the life of EI-Bira Mayor Ibrahim Taw'il by Jewish terrorists gave terrible evidence of the deterioration of Arab-Israeli relations on the West Bank. A wave of shock spread through the Palestinian community, while right-wingers in Gush Emunim and the National Religious Party expressed "understanding" and "enthusiasm" for the would-be assassins.[60] Peace Now immediately condemned the crime, and demanded the disarming of all of Rabbi Meir Kahane's followers and Gush Emunim members, and the swift investigation of what it saw as a "full-fledged terrorist underground."[61] Ze'ev Schiff, military correspondent for Ha'aretz, noted how the authorities were dragging their feet, and gave a prophetic warning: "When an underground begins to spill blood in operations on behalf of a certain idea, there is no end to it. At first, they hit Arabs who support the PLO, and then they hit Jews who express different opinions and propose, or work on behalf of, a compromise with the Palestinians."[62]

Peace Now mobilized about 40,000 people to call for the government's resignation after a week of protests outside the Prime Minister's office in Jerusalem. These protests clearly rattled Begin, after an incident in which a

---

58. *Ha'aretz*, August 18, 1980.
59. *Jerusalem Post*, May 8, 1980; *Ha'aretz*, May 28, 1980, June 3, 1980; *Davar*, June 3, 1980.
60. *Jerusalem Post*, June 4, 1980, *Ha'aretz*, June 3, 1980.
61. *Jerusalem Post*, June 3, 1980.
62. *Ha'aretz*, June 6, 1980.

Peace Now activist shouting for his resignation could be heard in the background as Begin was being interviewed on the radio. The police then came under "enormous pressure" from the Prime Minister's office to restrict the licensed demonstration, which they heeded—arresting and beating one demonstrator, Amos Arieli, and tearing down several placards.[63]

The turnout at the demonstration was not as large as had been hoped, reflecting a trend that had begun earlier that spring. One Peace Now activist admitted that the number was probably inflated, with "15-20,000" a more reliable estimate. The simultaneous demonstrations in three cities and the highway action also "didn't get enough people." It was the "beginning of the hard time" for Peace Now.[64] Was the public beginning to lose hope after too many unheeded protests? One movement representative, speaking at the rally, Yossi Ben-Artzi, addressed himself to the Israeli public "which has given up, believing nothing could help anymore." He declared that Peace Now's demonstrations proved to Jews in Israel and around the world and to Israel's supporters that there is "another Israel"— that the Israel they knew in the past still existed.[65] Such statements betray the growing sense of despair and polarization that was beginning to crystallize in Israel and affect Peace Now.

THE COLLAPSE OF PEACE NOW

From this point on, the movement stopped attempting big actions for several reasons. One was, as Janet Aviad, an academic who was then serving as its treasurer, told me a few years later, "people were tired, and it seemed we weren't getting anywhere. We did not have any new means to attack the problems..."[66] Rafi Greenberg, another Peace Now activist, added that,"In the summer everyone goes abroad. It is virtually impossible to move anyone." The fact that "people thought they could go away shows the loss of momentum" that had occurred, he noted.[67]

A second reason was that the political climate had changed. Dedi

---

63. *Jerusalem Post*, June 24, 1980.
64. Author interview with Rafi Greenberg, August 2, 1982.
65. *Jerusalem Post*, June 22, 1980.
66. Author interview with Janet Aviad, August 3, 1982.
67. Author interview with Rafi Greenberg, August 2, 1982.

Zucker recalled that, "The issue had become more and more the possibility of changing governments, and the negotiations over autonomy were frozen."[68] Public attention shifted to the political parties as they began to jockey for position. Begin's popularity was falling, and it seemed as though Labor was a shoo-in. A third reason was that there were fewer concrete provocations to respond to. Few settlements were established during the second half of 1980, and in any case many Peace Now leaders had recognized that they had lost the battle against the government's settlements policy.

Peace Now did take somewhat of an active position that fall on two legislative matters directly affecting the chances for peace: the "Jerusalem Law" affirming Israel's annexation of East Jerusalem and the proposed annexation of the Golan Heights. Both pieces of legislation were advanced by extreme right M.K. Geula Cohen (Tehiya Party) with the intention of closing off any chance of their ever being returned or even discussed in negotiations and thus, as the *Jerusalem Post*'s editorialist put it, sought "to blow the hope for peace to smithereens."[69] Most of the Labor Party coalition, with the exception of Yossi Sarid and Mapam party members and a few others, voted for the Jerusalem Law ostensibly because they agreed with its content (Jerusalem's unity under Israeli sovereignty). They also feared being seen as willing to redivide the city again. For falling into this right-wing trap, Labor was duly criticized by Peace Now and dovish M.K.s and newspapers.

The movement was also going through an internal crisis that prevented it from undertaking any major actions. There had always been conflicts among its leadership—primarily among the Jerusalem core group and secondarily between the Jerusalem and Tel Aviv branches. Such differences occurred because of personality conflicts or conflicts over leadership that were bound to happen. And disagreements over fine points of ideology had always been kept subservient to the task at hand—mobilizing public opposition to Begin and the Israeli right.

Many of the movement's leaders acknowledge that internal conflicts tended to rise when the leaders were not busy reacting to external events

---

68. Author interview with Dedi Zucker, August 18, 1982.
69. *Jerusalem Post*, July 29, 1980.

and organizing activities. With few exceptions, each of them also entertained possible political ambitions, a factor that added some tension to their interactions. Thus, as the creeping sense of frustration and impotence intensified during the spring and summer of 1980, the movement began to tear itself apart from the inside. As Moti Perry pointed out when I discussed this with him during one of our several conversations in early 1983, with the political atmosphere shifting towards the possibility of early elections, "there was not enough incentive to not fight internally."[70] Or as Zucker put it in a conversation that prior summer, "A different show was in town.[71]

More importantly, something of the original circle's internal balance was lost when Perry, Ariel Rubenstein and Tzali Reshef all left to study abroad in the fall of 1979. It was this group who, along with Zucker, Omri Padan, Abu Vilan, Yuli Tamir, Janet Aviad and a few others, had formed the nucleus of Peace Now. Despite certain inevitable and other perhaps unnecessary undemocratic features, the movement had effectively functioned through the consensus of this group. After Perry, Rubenstein, and Reshef left, their informal consensus-making process began to break down, with more unilateral initiatives being taken by various movement figures.

Two issues catalyzed the movement's internal disintegration and shutdown. One was an unofficial meeting between Zucker and Tamir and well-known PLO moderate Issam Sartawi in Europe, and the other was the upcoming elections. Because during the fall of 1980 the movement was already growing weaker due to the aforementioned combination of public apathy, political ineffectiveness, and internal conflict, it is difficult to say which of these three issues was the deciding factor. They show in vivid detail the internal vulnerability of an organization based solely on mutual trust, cooperation, and single-minded commitment to the risk of disruption and disintegration. Personal ambition and personality conflicts were two contributing factors, making the nucleus more brittle and susceptible to shattering. And internal mistrust and political antagonism could be masked in quarrels over politics very easily.[72]

---

70. Author interview with Moti Perry, January-February 1983.
71. Author interview with Dedi Zucker, August 18, 1982.
72. Author interview with Moti Perry, January-February 1983.

As Abu Vilan commented to me in the summer of 1982, "We knew that if you wanted to break the movement, just say to Israeli public opinion that we met with PLO leaders."[73] The unofficial meeting with Sartawi, an aide to Arafat who had already met before with many other left-wing Israelis, was a secret to the leadership for several months. But when others in the inner circle heard of the unsanctioned action by the two well-known Peace Now leaders, their reaction was angry and swift. People feared that Begin would use the fact of the meeting to destroy the movement's credibility. After several days of high-level internal discussions, Zucker and Tamir agreed to take the responsibility for what they had done upon themselves, and to withdraw for a few months.[74]

Many of the leaders acknowledged in retrospect that the movement was operating at a fraction of its height by that time. True, Peace Now had met with Labor Party officials to discuss their platform for the upcoming elections, and it continued to voice opposition to the proposed Golan annexation. Indeed, that fall, many internal discussions took place in the various branches of the movement in preparation for an upcoming ideological conference. The conference at Jerusalem's Binyinei Ha'uma hall attracted some two thousand supporters, all concerned with the question "What is to be done?" And as the *Jerusalem Post*'s reporter, Marsha Pomerantz, observed, most "left without an answer." As she wrote, "Peace Now represents a brand of humanism, but there are no very specific instructions for being human, or humane, in the Israel of 1980."[75]

Various committees reported on plans for more educational activity and outreach to young people, for making inroads in the Sephardi community, and so on. But with the elections seemingly around the corner, many of the activists were turning their attention towards political work on behalf of a party. The "Sartawi affair" had just broken two days before and many insiders knew the movement was in trouble.

According to Moti Perry, "It became clear that the movement couldn't function." He, Reshef, Rubenstein and Padan met in Princeton (where Perry was then studying), and decided that for the sake of preserving

---

73. Author interview with Abu Vilan, August 5, 1982.
74. Author interview with Moti Perry, January-February 1983.
75. *Jerusalem Post*, October 27, 1980.

Peace Now's name, they would announce that the movement would not enter politics as a party, and that it counseled its supporters to work for Peace Now's principles in the party that they personally preferred.[76] The movement's central forum met once, after a hiatus of several months, to confirm this decision and to agree that any of the leaders could join any political party, but that no one could do so in the movement's name.[77] Dedi Zucker and Yuli Tamir then joined the Citizen's Rights Movement, occupying the third and fourth positions of its list for the elections. Abu Vilan went to work on behalf of Mapam, Omri Padan for Labor, and Yossi Ben-Artzi to Shinui. Janet Aviad later told me, "I worked for two parties. I just had to do something then."[78]

Essentially, this final decision was a very wise and pragmatic one. Peace Now always faced the danger of an internal split if it tried to draw up a platform on the whole range of social, political and economic issues concerning Israelis, and so had wisely avoided fragmentation by remaining unified around the broad principles of the Officers' Letter, and by concentrating solely on the peace issue. More concretely, both its supporters and leaders had different opinions and loyalties to different parties. Any attempt to make Peace Now into a political party would have therefore failed, even if its leadership had not been bitterly fighting among themselves. By announcing to their supporters its withdrawal from the political arena, the movement's leaders managed to save the public image of Peace Now as a unified organization, a fact of inestimable value for its post-election revival.

---

76. Author interview with Moti Perry, January-February 1983.
77. Author interview with Dedi Zucker, August 18, 1982.
78. Author interview with Janet Aviad, August 3, 1982.

CHAPTER 5
FROM DESPAIR TO REBIRTH

FOR NEARLY ALL OF 1981, Peace Now was effectively moribund. But meanwhile another year of political upheaval began for both Israelis and the Palestinians of the occupied territories. Acts like the closing of Bir Zeit University and the final deportation of Mayors Kawasmeh and Milhem sparked demonstrations by Palestinian youth that were bloodily suppressed by Israeli soldiers. Sensing that its time was short, the Begin government renewed its settlement push in the West Bank. Kiryat Arba settlers continued to provoke Hebron's Arab population with intentional acts of vandalism and intimidation. Yet many observers saw this as evidence of the Begin government's lame-duck attempts to sabotage a future Labor government's peace strategy. No one expected a turnaround in Begin's fortunes.

It is worth going into more detail on two pre-election developments: the Likud's rise amid anti-Labor political violence, and Begin and Sharon's adventures in Iraq and Lebanon. Though both pre-date the war in Lebanon by a year, they show how the Israeli population was becoming more polarized, Begin and Sharon's willingness to exploit this polarization to their advantage, and their readiness to use the Israeli army for offensive purposes, capitalizing on the new strategic balance created by the peace treaty with Egypt. Though neither of these two developments could have had any immediate effect on Peace Now's perception of its role, they signal the arrival of what some Israelis since called the "real right"—a topic we will return to in greater detail.

In December of 1980, opinion polls showed the Labor Alignment receiving 30.2% of the electorate's support and the Likud only 18.7%. In January, this gap grew to 44.7% to 22.0%, with each party picking up support from undecided voters.[1] Yet on June 30, 1981, the Likud once again emerged victorious. What contributed to Begin's change in fortunes?

The free-spending policies of the new Minister of Finance Yoram Aridor definitely gave Begin a boost. In a series of policy shifts based more on political concerns than on good economic sense, Aridor announced a sizable increase in low-cost government loans for housing and a reduction on customs duties on luxury items and durables like small and medium-sized cars, color TVs, washing machines, and cameras. Shoppers flocked to the stores. This giveaway was financed by the spending of the entire 1981 budget for subsidies on goods and services (six billion shekels—about $428 million) within the first four months of the year. Public government bonds which usually sold for five to ten years with 3% interest were sold during March and April for two years at 7.5%. From May through July the treasury printed about 6.7 billion shekels, 65% of the amount budgeted for the year. While the opposition parties, the press, and many economists attacked these steps, the public literally ate them up. Inflation dipped slightly and private consumption increased by 4.5% in real terms. Though many of Aridor's moves were likely to have serious long-term effects, they achieved their purpose. In the short run, the handling of the economy became a secondary issue in the elections.[2]

A second factor contributing to Begin's rapid rise was his adventurist saber-rattling over the Syrian SAM missiles in Lebanon in mid-May and then his bold decision to destroy Iraq's Osirak atomic reactor in mid-June. Here was Begin the demagogue, creating instability and exploiting his tough stand's popularity with many Israelis, especially Sephardim.

The crisis with the Syrians developed when rightist Christian Phalange forces, long supplied by Israel, came to threaten Syria's main supply line from Damascus to Beirut (probably with Israeli encouragement). This led

---

1. *Ha'aretz*, January 2, 1981.
2. *Israleft News Service*, No. 184, March 8, 1981, p. 7 and No.191, August 20, 1981, p.7.

to a brutal Syrian counterattack and resupply operation which Israel disrupted, shooting down two Syrian helicopters to aid the Phalangists. At that point, the Syrians broke a five-year-old "gentleman's" agreement with Israel by moving SAM-6 missile batteries into Lebanon proper. Then Begin began to grandstand, warning the Syrians that if they did not remove the missiles then Israel would. The Syrian threat to Israeli control of Lebanon's airspace was supposedly at issue, but it was clear to some Israelis that Begin's brinkmanship had a domestic political source as well.

An important part of the background to the crisis was the thinly veiled Israeli interest in imposing a solution on Lebanon that would favor its Christian allies, and, more importantly, its interest in destroying the PLO's growing military infrastructure in Lebanon and hurting the Syrians. As the Syrian onslaught on the Christian population grew, so did the pretext for a direct Israeli intervention. Strategically, the timing could not have been much better from Israel's point of view. Syria was isolated in the Arab world, its support for Iran having aroused a conflict with Iraq and Jordan.

As it turned out, signals from the U.S. led Israel to accept a new round of Special Envoy Philip Habib's shuttling between Syria, Lebanon, and Israel. The Israeli threat gave the U.S. a bargaining card with which to urge the Saudis to pressure Syria to stop its shelling of Christian populations in Zahle and Beirut, and to withdraw its missiles. Israel also took advantage of the crisis to continue its airstrikes against Palestinian forces in southern Lebanon.

As the missile crisis peaked, some voices in Israel rose to protest the danger of war with the Syrians for less than necessary reasons. Writing in *Ha'aretz*, Yizhar Smilansky's words sound all too much like criticisms made by Israel's anti-war movement a year later. He warned that war could not solve the problem of the Syrian missiles. Calling on the citizenry to protest, he declared: "If we do not do something right away—war will break out. A war whose beginning may seem contained and controlled, but whose end —like all wars—we cannot predict. A war which even if we win it will change nothing. Except for the victims, except for the isolation, except for the eternal cycle of consequences wiping out initial gains which prove to have been illusory ... A war with no positive national goal, without a general national consensus, a war which does not remove the causes for the war—what is it for?"[3]

Criticism from the Labor opposition was timid and weak, due to its fear of appearing unpatriotic and because it basically approved of Begin's goals. It limited itself to hints that perhaps the crisis was due to Christian aggressiveness encouraged and abetted by Israel rather than Syrian war preparations. Fearing the possible outbreak of a clearly non-defensive war, a few Peace Now activists mainly affiliated with the Mapam party decided to break their moratorium on political activity and held a demonstration that attracted, at most, ten thousand people.[4]

The attack on the Syrian missiles was held up while U.S. envoy Habib attempted to defuse the crisis. In the meantime, Begin presented another fait accompli to the world: the destruction of Iraq's French-built atomic reactor. He justified the unilateral action by noting that the reactor was to become operational July 1 and that Iraq's Saddam Hussein had supposedly stated that the reactor was aimed at the Zionist enemy (a quote lacking any documentation). Thus, just as Begin had earlier argued that Israel must save the Lebanese Christians from a "holocaust" at the hands of the Syrians and Palestinians, he claimed that he had prevented a future holocaust against the Israeli people. He scoffed at world condemnation of Israel's violation of international law, reminding his people of how the world had stood by while the Jews suffered. In doing so, Begin expertly and quite unselfconsciously played on deep-rooted fears in segments of Israel's Jewish population (the so-called "fortress mentality"), and presented himself as their deliverer.

Suggestions from opposition leaders that perhaps the bombing of the reactor was politically motivated or ill-timed backfired because Begin was to make much political capital of those remarks. He explicitly demanded the same blind support for government decisions on the use of military force that he had always given Labor when he was in the opposition. Labor leaders refused and Begin went on the offensive—attacking them as disloyal, saboteurs, and collaborators with the enemy. His statements began to take on a euphoric and messianic manner, inflaming die-hard

---

3. *Ha'aretz*, May 10, 1981.
4. *New Outlook*, June 1981, p. 45.

Likud supporters to anti-Labor violence. Several Labor Party rallies were violently disrupted, and hundreds of Labor Party activists were physically intimidated; their car tires slashed if they exhibited a Labor Party bumper-sticker, their homes' windows smashed. Several Labor Party local offices were fire-bombed, but fortunately no one was hurt.[5]

The political violence of the campaign began to take on an explicitly ethnic character, based on deeply-rooted antagonisms between the larger and less well-off Sephardi Jews and the smaller but better-off Ashkenazi community. Whether the image was accurate or not, most of the public came to believe that the anti-Labor violence was coming from young Sephardi hoodlums inspired by Begin's rhetoric. Sensing that the public was threatened by this development, Labor leaders seized upon what they say as an opportunity to reverse their declining fortunes by stigmatizing the Likud as unruly and undemocratic.

The issue polarized Israel as never before, with thinly-veiled remarks by Labor leaders barely disguising their dislike of the Sephardi community for supposedly ruining the "nice Israel"—i.e., the Israel built by the Ashkenazi, upper-middle class. As one observer noted, "the dominant tones of the election were the emotionally charged issues of Begin vs. Peres, democracy vs. fascism, political violence vs political tolerance, continued progress of the Likud as opposed to going back to the old days of the Alignment: the growers of tomatoes against the throwers of tomatoes."[6]

Some worried about the danger of fascism in Israel. The results of a poll published in the magazine *Monitin* took on added significance in light of the phenomena of crowds of Likud-supporters chanting "Begin, King of Israel" at political rallies. It found that 18.1% of the population preferred some form of "undemocratic government" and that 40.8% felt that to strengthen Israel in face of its difficult problems "it is necessary to totally change the political regime in Israel" and wanted the rise of "a strong regime of leaders who will not be dependent on parties." A narrow plurality of 41.4% disagreed.[7]

The election of June 30 did not bode well for Peace Now for several

---

5. *Jerusalem Post,* June 16, 1981, June 17, 1981, June 18, 1981.
6. Asher Arian, "Elections 1981: Competitiveness and Polarization," *The Jerusalem Quarterly,* Fall 1981, p. 12.
7. *Jerusalem Post,* June 17, 1981; *Monitin,* February, 1981.

reasons. The re-election of Begin, with super-hawk Sharon now as his defense minister, could only mean the continued consolidation of the de facto annexation of the occupied territories. In addition, given Israel's investment in its Christian quasi-allies in Lebanon, and its interest in hurting both the PLO and the Syrians, there was bound to be more Israeli intervention in that troubled country. Last, but not least, Israeli military initiatives of the previous month and Begin's demagogic success in using them to manipulate and inflame Israeli public opinion showed that Peace Now was to be up against a far stronger Begin—more popular, more aggressive, and more determined.

Peace Now did not immediately reactivate itself after the elections. Many of its activists had worked very hard during the campaign period. There was a "mood of great despair," recalled Janet Aviad. "People had no strength." A group of activists met and decided to wait for the dust to settle. "We didn't know how the government would behave immediately and so we decided to wait," she told me.[8] Clearly, most people lacked the energy or the hope to go on. In the aftermath of two and a half years of fighting a losing battle over the West Bank, followed by the crushing reality of four more years of Begin and Sharon, one can understand their fatigue.

In the following months it was to become very clear what the new government had in mind. First, in early July, it returned to its policy of "preventive" strikes at Palestinian positions (including refugee camps) in Lebanon. After over a week of Israeli airstrikes, the Palestinian guerrillas responded with heavy shelling of Israeli border settlements. Israel then retaliated with a very bloody airstrike of the PLO's offices in Beirut proper. The midday attack killed approximately three hundred people and wounded another eight hundred, mostly innocent civilians. The Prime Minister's Office issued a statement announcing that population centers in Lebanon would no longer be spared.

With a full-scale war between the Israelis and the Palestinians on the verge of breaking out, world condemnation focused on Israel's actions.[9] The U.S. effectively pressured Israel to accept Habib's mediation, in part by extending its suspension of delivery of F-16 jets and threatening to "re-

---

8. Author interview with Janet Aviad, August 3, 1982.
9. *The Middle East Reporter*, Vol. 34, No. 217, July 18, 1981.

evaluate" its policy towards Israel. The strong response of the alerted and well-organized Palestinian militias, which successfully caused the mass exodus of some 20,000 Israeli civilians from northern settlements, may have also been a factor. The end-result of Begin's aggression, to his chagrin, was a fragile cease-fire effectively between Israel and the PLO (though it was negotiated through the U.S., the U.N., and Saudi Arabia).

As the hostilities abated, commentators in Israel pointed out the series of steps that had paradoxically led to the opposite result from what Begin wanted. Israel's international image was badly tarnished, the PLO' s infrastructure had emerged nearly unscathed and was given time to resupply and rebuild, and Israel's relations with the U.S. were battered. In an open letter signed by Peace Now activist Prof. Ze'ev Sternhell and others, the choice facing Begin was made clear: "[either] the occupation of southern Lebanon, taking the calculated risk of war with Syria, in order to keep the famous promise you made in Kiryat Shmona [that no more PLO Katyusha rockets will fall in that northern border town]; or political negotiations with the forces fighting in Lebanon order to lay the foundations for a general settlement in the area."

Sternhell called on Begin to recognize that he could not continue to use fear of "terrorism to solve the problems of Zionism," to uphold the IDF's concept of "purity of arms" and avoid striking civilian targets, and to use the ceasefire with the PLO as a bridge to peace.[10] At that time 60% of the Israeli public believed that there could be no comprehensive peace with the Arab states without a resolution of the Palestinian problem. But given Begin's ideological outlook and Israel's military superiority, everyone knew that the initiation of a full-scale invasion of southern Lebanon was just a matter of timing. The brave and clear-sighted call of a Peace Now man went unheeded. The movement itself as yet had not resurfaced.

The fact that Begin had no interest whatsoever in pursuing a peaceful resolution of the conflict was made even clearer by Israel's nearly instantaneous rejection of the Saudis' seven-point blueprint for peace and its behind-the-scenes efforts to force the U.S. to support this position.[11]

---

10. *Ha'aretz*, August 3, 1981.
11. Claudia Wright, "Strategy and Deception in Reagan's Policy Towards the Arabs," *Journal of Palestine Studies*, Spring 1982, p. 20.

Though from Israel's point of view Prince Fahd's plan was very harsh—calling for full withdrawal to the pre-1967 borders, removal of all settlements, repatriation or compensation of Palestinian refugees, and the establishment of an independent Palestinian state—it did offer "recognition of the right of all states in the region to live in peace."

Whether the Saudi proposal was intended mainly for U.S. consumption, as some observers noted, was irrelevant. Israel could have responded in a cautiously positive manner to test the Saudis' intentions. But the appearance of a real shift in Saudi Arabia's policy towards Israel might have set off a process leading to Arab moderation and the strengthening of anti-annexationist forces within Israel, both developments that could weaken Begin's hold on the West Bank. Therefore his rejection of the Saudi plan was immediate, total and unconditional.[12] It should be added that many hawks in Labor supported Begin's response.

LIBERALIZATION, SHARON-STYLE, ON THE WEST BANK

The most important series of developments of the fall of 1981 in Israel pertained to Defense Minister Ariel Sharon's so-called "new look" in the occupied territories. Sharon, the man who ruthlessly "pacified" the Gaza Strip a decade earlier, who was known for his military daring and insensitivity to human life (even that of his own soldiers) was talking of liberalizing Israel's control over the Palestinian population. A year earlier, when Sharon first began campaigning for Ezer Weizman's old job of Defense Minister, Deputy Prime Minister Simcha Ehrlich confidentially told the *Jerusalem Post*: "Arik Sharon is one of the politicians in Israel whom I fear as a danger to the state. Sometimes I tremble at what he might do if he had the chance." In a private "joke" with Ehrlich, Begin reportedly referred to the man he usually called his "favorite general" as capable of putting a ring of tanks around the Prime Minister's Office if he ever became Defense Minister. And in arguing for his succession to that post, Sharon was

---

12. *The Middle East Reporter*, Vol. 35, No. 220, August 8, 1981; New Outlook, September/October 1981, p. 5.

reputed to have said that "security is more important than the constitution."[13] What exactly did Sharon have in mind for the West Bank?

First it was announced in early August that harassment of Arabs at roadblocks, collective punishment and the entry of soldiers into schools would cease. An earlier order prohibiting West Bankers from making pro-PLO statements and barring West Bank municipalities from receiving funds from a committee jointly supervised by the PLO and Jordan, was left standing, however. Sharon was clearly looking to encourage the emergence of the mythical "moderate" Palestinian leadership to join the Camp David peace process, scheduled to resume that September. The logic of his strategy was clearly outlined in a May 1981 article in *Commentary* magazine by Hebrew University Professor Menachem Milson (soon to be appointed head of the West Bank's civilian administration) entitled "How to Make Peace with the Palestinians."

In brief, Milson argued that the autonomy talks had failed to attract the participation of pro-PLO mayors in the territories because "the PLO had come to control the political public" there and because it had unconditionally rejected the Camp David accords. The latter assertion he based on various public statements by PLO leaders from Arafat on down. The former condition he blamed on Israeli laxity vis-a-vis early expressions of anti-Israel radicalism, and on Israel's failure to cultivate a moderate leadership elite through patronage, as the Jordanians had done. Indeed, he attacked Israeli policy-makers for having allowed the flow of "PLO patronage money" into the West Bank, and for not having protected moderates from PLO terror and intimidation.

The result of these errors, he argued, was that the PLO had achieved "the unanimous support of the people." He dismissed entirely the possibility that Israel's settlements, land expropriations, and repressive control over the Palestinians had helped cause this outcome. But, he added, "This situation was not inevitable, and is not irreversible." The path toward some sort of Jordanian option was to be found "by freeing the population of the territories from the grip of the PLO." One can see why it was Milson who earlier advocated the establishment and financial and political support of Palestinian "village leagues." Unfortunately, Milson failed to realize that

---

13. *Jerusalem Post*, June 9, 1980; *Yediot Aharonot*, June 11, 1980.

any attempt to delegitimize the PLO would be seen as a direct attack on Palestinian nationalism and resisted as such.

Milson included a caveat designed to entice President Reagan's support. He argued that the West Bank's rejection of the Camp David accords was the key factor in preventing the formation of a pro-U.S. alliance of Egypt, Jordan, and Saudi Arabia. The latter two were hamstrung by the PLO's domination of the occupied territories, which prevented the possible acceptance of Camp David by these two countries. Thus, he wrote, "The way for the U.S. to help is not to demand further concessions from Israel in order to satisfy the PLO," but to support Israel's "campaign against PLO domination in the territories." Though Reagan's anti-Sovietism certainly had a role to play in the forthcoming September U.S.-Israel "strategic cooperation" agreement, clearly Israel's eagerness for the agreement betrayed its desire for U.S. approval for Milson's plan to rekindle the stalled Camp David talks, particularly in light of world-wide and especially Palestinian support for the Saudi plan.[14]

Milson's ideas about a moderate (i.e., anti-PLO) Palestinian leadership were fatally flawed. Palestinian mayors popularly elected in the 1975 elections remained stalwart in their demand for a Palestinian state led by the PLO. Thus, the November establishment of the civilian administration on the West Bank was viewed by Palestinians as another guise for hastening the annexation. November 2, "Balfour Day" for Palestinians, was marked as always by student demonstrations, disturbances, tire-burning, and stone throwing against Israeli vehicles and security forces. Pitched battles between youthful demonstrators and Israeli soldiers firing tear gas took place at Bir Zeit University and in Bethlehem.[15]

The "get-tough" side of Sharon and Milson's plan for encouraging Palestinian moderation was demonstrated by the imposition of curfews in the towns of Kalkilya and Beit Sahur, and by arrests, travel restrictions, and house arrests. Bir Zeit University, a focus of Palestinian nationalist activities, was closed down by the order of Milson and fifty Israelis demonstrating in Ramallah in opposition were teargassed.[16] The height of this

---

14. Menachem Milson, "How to Make Peace with the Palestinians," *Commentary*, May 1981, pp. 25-35.
15. *Ha'aretz*, November 3, 1981.
16. *Ha'aretz*, November 12, 1981.

new wave of repressive measures came when Sharon decided to blow up the homes of several youths from Beit Sahur who were suspected of throwing firebombs at Israeli vehicles.

Such a rarely-used punishment was reserved generally for homes in which weapons or explosives had been found or prepared. The Israeli government maintained that it would continue aiding the "peace-loving population" in the territories (i.e. the village leagues) while opposing violent actions which harmed Jews or Arabs. Critics decried the excessive use of force and the resulting radicalization of some Palestinians formerly thought "very moderate."

PEACE NOW REVIVES ITSELF

The closing of Bir Zeit University and the destruction of homes in Beit Sahur were precipitating events stimulating public protest in Israel. In the absence of a massive movement like Peace Now, other groups filled the vacuum, albeit inadequately. A group calling itself the Israeli Committee for Solidarity with Bir Zeit University organized many small but significant protest demonstrations—calling for the opening of the university and the establishment of a Palestinian state alongside Israel.[17] Other groups explicitly espousing that solution advertised statements calling for an end to the occupation and the repression.

Clearly, the violence surrounding Begin's re-election and the awareness that the Likud was probably going to be around for a while was beginning to radicalize some Israelis. But this opposition was weak and small. Even with Gush Emunim and Tehiya organizing a "Movement to Stop the Retreat from Sinai" and then Begin's sudden annexation of the Golan Heights in December, a relatively moderate group like the Mapam party could only muster 1,500 people for a demonstration opposing Begin's action. There was no paucity of press criticism of these developments but there was also barely any public response. Where was Peace Now?

The movement was in the first stages of reorganization at this time. It was in part weakened by the absence of key leaders like Dedi Zucker, Yuli Tamir, Omri Padan, Tzali Reshef, and Ariel Rubenstein, who were all

---

17. *Israleft News Service*, No. 196, December 7, 1981, p. 2.

outside the country. In a way, though, their very absence allowed new leaders to intentionally restructure the movement from the start along more open and democratic lines. A key person in this renaissance of Peace Now was Janet Aviad, a sociologist in Jerusalem who was the movement's treasurer during what she and others had begun to call "the first round." When we met in August of 1982, she described the first tentative steps they took: "We started with little meetings in my apartment where everyone came full of doubts ... Everyone knew that there must be a public voice in the street, especially in light of the Labor Party's [post-elections] collapse ... The question was if the timing was right and if there was going to be a second generation [of fresh support for Peace Now] ... and if the framework should be Peace Now or if we should start a new form free of its historical burdens."[18]

The initial months were spent in discussions on the purpose and framework of activities to be taken, and by small symbolic steps that began to put Peace Now back in the public eye and also served to galvanize its activists. In November, about forty people went to visit Beit Sahur to see the results of Israel's renewed policy of collective punishment. For Aviad, "that was the red light." She continued her story: "By December, the situation on the West Bank was degenerating rapidly ... The de facto annexation of the West Bank was proceeding at a great pace, the settlements were expanding enormously with government backing. [Milson's] firing of the mayors [in March 1982] really spurred us on to [our] first demonstration which put us back on the map."

The early months of 1982 brought little good news to Israeli doves. Israel's December annexation of the Golan Heights planted another obstacle to territorial compromise with the Arabs and only confirmed impressions of Israel as expansionist. Unlike the West Bank, Begin's party had no ideological claim to the Heights, and clearly sought to strengthen Arab rejectionists and weaken the moderates—particularly with the Saudis' proposal gaining acceptance. Similarly, one can interpret Israel's insistence that Egyptian President Hosni Mubarak come to Jerusalem as a stalling tactic meant to avoid the reopening of the autonomy question until

---

18. Author interview with Janet Aviad, August 3, 1982.

Sharon, Milson, et. al. had wiped out the PLO's influence in the occupied territories.

Bright spots, like the January calls of Bethlehem Mayor Elias Freij and Gaza Mayor Rashad Shawa urging the PLO to recognize Israel and struggle politically for a state were ignored by PLO leaders set on building their military infrastructure and distrustful of Israeli intentions, especially in southern Lebanon. The Israeli press began to report that Israel was indeed preparing a full-scale invasion.[19] Topping it off, the "Movement to Prevent the Retreat from Sinai" was daily filling the Israeli media with wrenching scenes of soldiers confronting religious militants, some who threatened to commit suicide rather than leave Sinai. And on the West Bank, Gush Emunim settlers continued their harassment of Palestinians.

Roni Siegel, a new activist who had joined the circle in Jerusalem, described one of the movement's reactions to the worsening situation: "One of the first things we did in Peace Now, one that motivates me, was that we went to Hebron, to the house of a woman who had grenades thrown at her by settlers from Kiryat Arba. About one hundred people went ... The visit's purpose was partly to foster better relations, and partly to say there is another Israel that does care ... that is not out to take your land ... that believes there is another way, that violence is not the solution."[20]

The demonstration was successful in bringing the movement publicity. Adding to the movement's revitalization, Tzali Reshef and Ariel Rubenstein returned home from their studies in the U.S. in January, and that was "very, very, important," according to Janet Aviad. "Then we started to meet. Every weekend three or four people met until we got straight what we wanted to do and how to do it."[21] It seems that no one really believed the movement could return to the days when it had rallied thousands. When Reshef returned and told his friends that he planned to go back to his Peace Now activities, for example, they told him, "Confused boy—that business fell apart a while ago."[22]

Though the movement was beginning to strengthen organizationally, it

---

19. *New York Times*, January 23, 1982; January 25, 1982, February 10, 1982.
20. Author interview with Roni Siegel, August 2, 1982.
21. Author interview with Janet Aviad, August 3, 1982.
22. *Ha'aretz*, March 28, 1982.

had still not chosen a focus for major action. In the early months of 1982 both the repression on the West Bank and the danger that the "Movement to Prevent the Retreat from the Sinai" would successfully prevent the last stage of the Israeli withdrawal occupied their attention. As Aviad reflected, "We knew that in the end our problem was the West Bank. But we knew in the meantime it might be useful to have Peace Now on the map in case a large national movement was needed to oppose the movement against withdrawal from Sinai."[23]

For most of February and March, the movement's leaders withheld from taking any steps to protest the actions of the ultra-nationalists in Sinai, primarily because it appeared that the government had every intention of honoring the treaty with Egypt and because they did not want to give Begin a pretext to support the anti-withdrawal movement. As long as the government's commitment held firm, they had no reason to get involved.

But then, as Aviad put it, "The killing of the little kids on the West Bank started."[24] Palestinian resistance to the new civilian administration had continued unabated through the winter. Crowds of young Palestinians would gather to denounce the occupation, wave the Palestinian flag, and stone Israeli troops and vehicles. Increasingly, troops resorted to firing into the crowds to force them to disperse (and sometimes continued firing after they had begun to do so), killing and wounding dozens. Many of the victims were teenagers. In mid-March, Milson's administration took the additional step of removing the duly elected pro-PLO mayors of El Bireh, Nablus, and Ramallah from office (referred to above by Aviad), blaming them for the violence of the demonstrators.[25] The nightly television reports showing Israeli troops firing into crowds of Palestinian protesters clearly began to shock and outrage a broad segment of Israeli society. It soon became obvious to the leaders of the movement that regardless of the public response, they had to act.

"With great hesitation, we decided to take a chance—because if we didn't protest this, then we have no right to be," said Aviad. They feared

---

23. Author interview with Janet Aviad, August 3, 1982.
24. Ibid.
25. *The New York Times*, March 25, 1982.

that a small turnout would mean the real death of Peace Now, and they had no idea how many Israelis would be moved to protest the much more controversial and fundamental issue of Israel's occupation of the West Bank. "We talked about a success as 5,000 (people], nothing more," recalled Abu Vilan.[26] Aviad described her recollection of this first, perhaps fatal, step: "We organized in a very non-professional way. The telephone network was dead ... people had moved. So, we did it by ads in the newspapers ... That morning it started to pour and hail. And we said, 'okay, there will be two hundred people there and that's the end of Peace Now.' 30,000 showed up ... we were flabbergasted."[27]

The movement was not timid in its choice of slogans. The main one for this demonstration stated: "Policies of annexation and perpetual control over another people lead to tyranny and corruption." It also attacked recent government pressure on the inhabitants of the newly annexed Golan Heights to accept Israeli identity papers. But the main focus of Peace Now speakers was the moral issue of the occupation.

Tzali Reshef asserted that "people don't get killed by accident. We don't like things like this done in our name." From a religious perspective, Professor Uriel Simon declared that, "The love of the land of Israel without the love of man is dangerous. We must remember that all men, not only the children of Israel, were created in God's image."[28] Janet Aviad also spoke of her concern for Israel's moral character: "The issue was very important. We said very clearly: the occupation brings bloodshed ...The implication is that it corrupts our moral standards ... when people are no longer shocked when fifteen kids get shot in two weeks, then something is very deeply the matter ... and we have to demonstrate that there is another Israel that will not be quiet about it.[29] Many of the placards held by the crowd read "The army is for defense, and not shooting at demonstrations," and in a reference to South Africa, "Cry, the beloved country."

Two isolated incidents were blown totally out of proportion by politicians and the conservative press. Someone demonstrated with a sign depicting the Israeli flag and a Palestinian flag side-by-side, and another

---

26. Author interview with Abu Vilan, August 5, 1982.
27. Author interview with Janet Aviad, August 3, 1982.
28. *Al Ha'Mishmar*, March 28, 1982.
29. Author interview with Janet Aviad, August 3, 1982.

person with a placard reading "the Golan is Syrian." (Both were taken down by organizers of the rally.) Most of the state television's coverage focused on the "Palestinian flag" incident, making the demonstration seem more radical than it was. Some Peace Now leaders saw this as a deliberate attempt to "sabotage" their movement by "adding people to the category of those that won't listen."[30]

Prime Minister Begin jumped on them for it, calling them "spoiled fruit" and raising the possibility of investigating Peace Now's ties to Palestinian organizations. Several hawks in Labor joined him in attacking the movement, turning on the doves within their party who had supported the protest. Faced with the equivalent of red-baiting, Peace Now was forced to openly rebut the accusation and reassert their Zionist credentials. The movement's spokesman, Tzali Reshef, pointedly attacked Begin for using the incident "to divert public attention away from the horrible results of his policies." In the final analysis, the "Palestinian flag" incident probably hurt Peace Now mainly in the electorate already beholden to Begin by adding to their impression of the movement as "Arab lovers" and "Arafatists."[31]

This first demonstration was very significant. For one, twenty-six members of Knesset had publicly supported it, including several who usually did not identify themselves as doves. This number was more than for any earlier Peace Now demonstration. Moreover, the demonstration showed that Peace Now had never lost its appeal. "The name carried power and not just on the basis of its actual record," observed Janet Aviad. "For some reason, for a lot of Israelis the name had a kind of charismatic power," which a new group would have had to rebuild. Some activists saw their support as coming from the same 100,000 people who had come to the movement's biggest rally on the eve of Camp David.

Many others, like Rafi Greenberg, believed that Peace Now was attracting a "second generation" of supporters. Many of its supporters in the "first round" had explained that the basis of their activism was their desire not to fight in another war after the 1973 cataclysm, and especially not an avoidable war. In contrast, it seems likely that this "second genera-

---

30. Author interview with Rafi Greenberg, August 2, 1982.
31. *Ha'aretz*, March 30, 1982 and April 1, 1982.

tion" was politicized more by Begin's extremism and the ominous danger of what in Israel was being broadly spoken of as fascism.[32]

The significance of this first demonstration is underlined by the fact that, afterwards, the movement "took off everywhere." In Tel Aviv, what used to be a relatively weak branch of Peace Now began to regularly draw 250 people to its bi-weekly general meetings, and a telephone network of over one thousand hard-core supporters was quickly set up.[33] The Jerusalem branch had more than 1,600 people on its telephone network by this time. Activists were occupied with the mundane but essential details of clarifying organizational processes, setting up various outreach programs, and planning new actions.[34]

At the same time, about seventy to one-hundred Peace Now activists from around the country met at Kibbutz Ga'ash to hammer out the movement's platform and discuss strategy. The result was a two-page position paper called "Amdateinu" ("Our Stand"), which reaffirmed many of Peace Now's earlier stands. The position paper went further than these earlier statements in attacking the occupation and calling for a peace agreement with the Palestinians. Some of its highlights were: a call for readiness by "both sides to agree to a partition in the land of Israel," the recognition of "Palestinian national existence," a repetition of Peace Now's call for an Israeli initiative to break "the vicious cycle of Israeli-Palestinian hostility," and a condemnation of Begin's attempt to use the autonomy plan "as a vehicle for annexation and as an obstacle to any future peace agreements."

It demanded an immediate moratorium on settlement and expropriation of land on the West Bank, the restraining of the settlers, the lifting of restrictions placed on the Arab population there ("the right of these residents to manage their own affairs and maintain their own institutions should be preserved"), and the redirection of all Israeli resources currently channeled towards settlements towards solving "the problems of the social gap and of deprivation within Israel."[35]

For the rest of the spring, Peace Now kept its attention focused on the

32. *Ha'aretz*, March 28, 1982; Author interviews with Janet Aviad and Rafi Greenberg, August 2 and 3, 1982.

33. Author interview with Tami Tzarfati, August 10, 1982.

34. Author interviews with lta Gibson, July 20, 1982, and Roni Siegel, August 2, 1982.

35. Peace Now pamphlet, June 1982.

West Bank. The Israeli government had completed the withdrawal from Sinai on schedule, though many believed that it had deliberately encouraged the resulting emotional and traumatic spectacle to impress the public with the impossibility of withdrawing from any other settlements. In any case, after the withdrawal, Defense Minister Sharon pledged that it would be Israel's last territorial concession for peace and promised a new drive to expand Jewish settlement on the West Bank and Gaza.[36] The public was invited to Independence Day dedication ceremonies for several new settlements. Little did Sharon expect the surprise Peace Now had planned for him.

Several hundred demonstrators converged on the ceremonies at a settlement called Telem where Sharon was to appear. Those who managed to get in disrupted his speech, shouting slogans like "No [settlement] to the West Bank, Yes to the Arava [the Negev desert]," getting TV coverage while being beaten up by right-wingers. A larger group that was prevented from attending the ceremonies at a nearby roadblock was teargassed. In this case the movement successfully used the media to make its point, choosing a symbolic action that might have alienated some Israelis because they were disrupting what was supposed to be a celebration, but instead caused the movement to be seen as "more serious."[37]

The movement also continued its attempts to focus protest on the bloodshed on the West Bank. There had been little let-up in Israel's repression of Palestinian nationalist demonstrations, and several more youths were killed or wounded by Israeli troops. A motion of no confidence in the Knesset over the government's handling of the disorders had resulted in a tie—prompting Begin to offer to resign. His cabinet convinced him not to do so.[38] Army authorities took no measures to alleviate the bloodshed. Later evidence showed that it was encouraged from the very top.

In response, a news conference of six reserve officers was held under the auspices of Peace Now. Citing twenty-four cases of brutality and collective punishment that they themselves had witnessed during their regular reserve service on the West Bank, the officers attacked the breakdown in

---

36. *The New York Times*, April 26, 1982.
37. Author interviews with Shaul Markowitz, August 3, 1982, and Janet Aviad, August 3, 1982.
38. *The New York Times*, March 24, 1982.

army discipline known in Israel as "the purity of arms." One specific complaint asserted that a lieutenant-colonel beat up the family of a boy shot dead by a Kiryat Arba settler when they tried to take his body away for burial. Others spoke of officers ordering their men to provoke and then beat Palestinians, of soldiers using clubs on innocent bystanders.[39] They also attacked the situation in which green, inexperienced conscripts were sent to disperse demonstrations lacking non-lethal, anti-personnel weapons and therefore forced to shoot at demonstrators.

The news conference had a great impact, particularly on the army. Activist Roni Siegel recalled it as:

> "...the most effective thing Peace Now has ever done. We relied on the Peace Now tradition of soldiers saying, 'their way is not our way.' The message was the cost of the occupation on the national character. The concept of "purity of arms" got much media coverage, and it led to the army stressing it in its internal education as well. Most importantly, we were preserving the character of a popular army. The conference led to a court of inquiry, which showed that people are to be held accountable for their actions, not that when you put on a uniform you are anonymous."[40]

Though the results of that inquiry into the alleged brutality of eight particular soldiers was to be obscured by the conclusions of the Kahan Commission's inquiry into the Sabra and Shatila massacre (which occurred later that year in Lebanon), it is worth noting some of the evidence unearthed for what it shows about the official military policy on the West Bank that spring. The defendants claimed that their actions were in accordance with directives from Defense Minister Sharon and Chief of Staff Eitan. According to their testimony, Sharon had told Menachem Milson that, when confronting demonstrators, troops should "seize their testicles and tear them off." They told of instances where they had been ordered to "hassle the population" by rounding up males between the ages of 18 and 25 to be taken to a local school to be beaten up. They gave examples of punitive arrests, cases of forced labor, and told of an incident where

---

39. *Middle East International*, January 7, 1983, p. 4.
40. Author interview with Roni Siegel, August 2, 1982.

soldiers had hijacked a school bus returning pupils to their homes and driven them to a remote spot and made the children walk home. The point was that these actions were not irregularities—they were consistent parts of a heavy handed policy of harassment, incitement, and brutality.[41] The soldiers all received light sentences. Peace Now had only scratched the surface.

In late May, Peace Now was continuing its protests over the government's West Bank policy. Forums were held, copies of "Amdateinu" distributed to the public, and petitions were collected totaling some 20,000 signatures. In early June, the movement was planning to hold a demonstration on the eve of a planned trip by Begin to the U.S.[42] The government, and Ariel Sharon in particular, had other plans.

---

41. *Middle East International*, January 7, 1983, p. 4.
42. *Jerusalem Post*, May 24, 1982 and May 30, 1982.

CHAPTER 6
THE 1982 WAR IN LEBANON AND AFTERMATH

ON JUNE 4, 1982, members of a radical Palestinian fringe group attempted to assassinate Israel's Ambassador to Britain Shlomo Argov. In retaliation, waves of Israeli jets attacked Palestinian strongholds in and around Beirut, provoking a Palestinian artillery barrage into northern Israel. Though on June 5 the PLO agreed to a U.N. Security Council call for a ceasefire and British authorities announced that the attempt on Argov's life was clearly the work of Syrian-backed, anti-Arafat, Abu Nidal group, Israel had its pretext in hand. The next day, it began a full-scale invasion of Lebanon—an invasion that within four days brought the Israeli army to the outskirts of Beirut amid untold death, destruction, and suffering.[1]

It is not my purpose here to examine and evaluate Israel's conduct of the war, the many assertions and counter-assertions about the war's toll, or the complex negotiations surrounding the PLO's departure from Beirut. But in terms of understanding the role of Peace Now during this period in Israel's history however, one must look at certain aspects of the war, most notably Begin and Sharon's political and strategic purposes and their justi-fication of the war to Israeli public opinion, to place an examination of Peace Now's reactions in perspective.

In focusing on the politics of protest during wartime, it's also important

---

1. *The New York Times*, June 4-7, 1982; *Village Voice*, June 22, 1982.

to note that several smaller but significant protest groups sprang up and gained popular support. Having personally been in Israel during the war, spending the summer living on a kibbutz on the border with Lebanon, I could add my own protest to the many that will follow, but I prefer to let their words stand on their own.

Why did Israel invade southern Lebanon? The stated intention of the men who called it "Operation Peace for Galilee" was to push the Palestinian forces in southern Lebanon 25 miles north so that they would no longer be able to shell Israel's northern settlements. They insisted that Israel would not engage Syria's forces in Lebanon unless Syrians engaged Israelis. At first the invasion appeared to command the support of a large majority of Israelis, though even from the very beginning voices of protest were raised. As the war developed and the reality of what the army was actually doing began to sink In, the tide of protest rose.

In the first few days, Israel and Syria engaged in tremendous air and armor battles. Israel battled Palestinians to the outskirts of Beirut, and Palestinian strongholds and refugee camps were pounded by Israel from the air, sea, and ground. A cease-fire between the two was broken by Israel, which then sealed off Palestinian-held West Beirut. Eleven days after the invasion, Begin left for the U.S., seeking Reagan's support for his newly-announced goals of achieving a stable, Christian-led, unified Lebanese government and the withdrawal of the embattled PLO from Lebanon.

While negotiations between Palestinian, Lebanese, and American officials started to get under way, Israeli forces embarked on a large-scale offensive to control the strategic Beirut-Damascus highway, breaking another Syrian-Israeli cease-fire. A drawn-out siege of West Beirut then began and lasted for most of July and August—punctuated by murderous and indiscriminate Israeli shelling, sometimes lasting twelve hours at a time, and slow advances into the city proper—and finally ending with the evacuation of the PLO fighters in the third week of August. It was a rapid assault in stages followed by a merciless war of attrition that went far beyond Begin's original stated objectives.

More critical observers began to discern that this was a war not only against the PLO, but against the very idea of Palestinian nationalism, that not only was it meant to create a "new order" in Lebanon, but that it also sought to perpetuate the old order of the occupation of the West Bank and the Gaza Strip. In the decade preceding the invasion, Israeli planners had come to believe that the military balance would probably eventually favor the Arabs qualitatively as well as quantitatively. From whence grew both the desire of many pragmatic doves to negotiate a resolution of the conflict with the Palestinians from a position of strength, and the contrasting decision of Begin and Sharon to act to radically alter the regional balance.

Why then did Israel attack in June of 1982? Professor Yehoshua Porat, writing in *Ha'aretz*, saw the decision as based on the implications of the year-long cease-fire between Israel and the PLO. The danger to Israel, and particularly to Begin's Greater Israel (as well as to all Israelis opposed to a Palestinian state), was that Arafat's success in adhering to the cease-fire was increasing the perception of the PLO as a legitimate international actor.[2] Israel was the first to violate the truce on April 21 when it bombed Palestinian positions south of Beirut after an Israeli soldier was killed by a land-mine in southern Lebanon. Arafat recognized the attack as an ambush intended to give Israel an excuse to invade, and so he decided not to retaliate.[3] Thus, as Porat pointed out, Israel needed a terrorist attack to occur to justify a massive retaliation that would force the PLO into a war. As was the case, Argov's assailants were arch enemies of Arafat's mainstream Fatah organization, but their attack provided the justification Israel was waiting for.

A legitimized PLO, particularly one that the U.S. was willing to deal with, if not recognize, posed a grave threat to Begin and Sharon. Their voiced concern at the threat the PLO's growing military infrastructure in southern Lebanon represented to Israel's security was shown to be a lie by the overwhelming nature of Israel's military victory itself. Rather, the key to their concern was their perception of the intimate link between the PLO and Palestinian militancy within the occupied territories.

Ze'ev Schiff, military correspondent for *Ha'aretz*, predicted on May 23 that Sharon would invade Lebanon because he believed "that quiet on the West Bank cannot be achieved merely by dismissing [Palestinian mayors] Shaka and Khalaf, but rather by the destruction of the PLO in Lebanon.[4] In

---

2. *Ha'aretz*, June 25, 1982.

3. *New York Times*, April 22, 1982; April 23, 1982.

4. *Ha'aretz*, May 23, 1982.

other words, Milson's plan to free the West Bank Palestinians from the domination of the PLO required a military operation against the PLO itself.[5] Other evidence of this campaign against Palestinian nationalism was found in Israel's post-battle removal and/or destruction of Palestinian cultural sources like research libraries in Beirut. In addition, indirect evidence surfaced of an Israeli plan to use the pretext of war to expel the West Bank Palestinians.[6]

The second hidden strategic goal had to do with Israel's (and particularly Sharon's) grand design for the Middle East. Recognizing that they lacked strategic depth, Israeli strategists from David Ben-Gurion on down had based their defense planning on sophisticated intelligence and the readiness to launch a preemptive strike in order to carry the fighting to enemy soil. This doctrine, Ben-Gurion emphasized, was operable only in the "no-choice" situation where Israel's existence was plainly at stake.[7] Interestingly, this was the argument that Begin attempted to make in justifying the war's ferocity. He suggested that acting against the PLO while the imbalance between them favored Israel would, in effect, save Israeli lives.[8] (The many parallels to Israel's decision to wage all-out war against Hamas after the October 7, 2023 attack, with little to no regard for Palestinian civilians in Gaza, and with the deliberate destruction as well of many Gazan universities, schools and hospitals, should be obvious.) And given Begin's ideological intransigence on the Palestinian question, it may be that this war effectively delayed the next one five or ten years.

The significance of Sharon's grand design was that it carried this preemptive concern from a defensive to a truly imperial level, consummating earlier hesitant steps taken by Labor government defense planners. In Sharon's own words, "Israel's security interests are affected by developments and events far beyond the area of direct confrontation upon which Israel has concentrated her attention in the past: In other words, beyond the Arab countries in the Middle East and on the shores of the Mediterranean and the Red Sea, we must expand the field of Israel's strategic and security concerns in the 1980's to include countries like Turkey, Iran,

---

5. Walid Khalidi, *Conflict and Violence in Lebanon*, p. 124.
6. *Ha'aretz*, May 23, 1982.
7. *Ha'aretz*, June 27, 1982.
8. *Jerusalem Post*, August 20, 1982.

Pakistan, and areas like the Persian Gulf and Africa, and in particular the countries of North and Central Africa."[9]

Revisionist ideologue Eri Jabotinsky (son of Begin's mentor Vladimir Jabotinsky) had from before Israel's establishment called for Zionism to work for "an alliance of minorities in the Middle East." The argument was that Israel's security lay in the weakening of Arab unity through the support of religious and ethnic minorities in all these countries. Labor governments shied away from fully exploiting the idea, though they did aid the Kurdish rebels in Iraq and then the Christian Phalange in Lebanon. It seems that Sharon took the possibilities of this "alliance of minorities" fully to heart."[10]

It's possible that in his wildest dreams Sharon hoped the war would not only be the final step in the creation of a Christian-led "pro-Western government with which Israel could sign a peace treaty," but also the first step in the destabilization of the Syrian and Jordanian regimes, and the eventual creation of a Palestinian Jordan (and consolidation of an Israeli West Bank) due to the influx of Palestinian refugees from Lebanon and the West Bank and Gaza.[11] At minimum his objectives were "a blow at the PLO to protect Galilee and to assure future control of Judea and Samaria; a blow at the Syrian missiles; and the implementation of the alliances of minorities philosophy, to create a Jerusalem-Cairo-Beirut peace triangle."[12]

The support of the U.S. was the necessary linchpin for such a strategy, and Sharon was well aware of America's ability to foil his plans, as it had curtailed Israel's invasion of southern Lebanon in the spring of 1978. Therefore, it was necessary to sell the idea of the PLO and their Syrian quasi-allies as pawns of the Soviets to the U.S., describing them as intent on building their capacity to interfere with U.S. plans for the Middle East. An eager buyer for this theory was found in U.S. Secretary of State Alexander Haig, who, after meeting with Begin in April of 1981 told of a U.S.-Israel

---

9. *Ma'ariv*, December 18, 1981; translated in the *Journal of Palestine Studies*, Spring 1982, p. 168-169.

10. *Jerusalem Post International Edition*, February 13-19, 1983, p. 12.

11. Amnon Kapeliuk, "Eliminating the Palestinian Roadblock—Toward a New Regional Order," *Le Monde Diplomatique*, July 1982; translated in *Journal of Palestine Studies*, Summer/Fall 1982, p. 289.

12. *Jerusalem Post International Edition*, February 13-19, 1982, p. 12.

"convergence of outlook in the area of broad, strategic threat to the Middle East region, to include traditional military threats from unfriendly super-powers, to include assessments of Soviet proxy [i.e. PLO] activity, and to include some very important discussions on the overall issue of international terrorism."[13]

After the abortive Israel-PLO war of the summer of 1981, and then the U.S.' decision to provide Saudi Arabia with AWACS surveillance aircraft, Israeli planners openly spoke of their receding "qualitative edge" and the need to invade Lebanon considering the PLO's Soviet-supplied growth in military strength. It appears that Sharon even advocated invading before the Sinai withdrawal was completed on April 25 (recall the "ambush" air attack of April 21) to forestall the loss of Sinai. The U.S. rewarded Israel's restraint in holding to the treaty with "confidence-building" measures like increased F-16 jet fighter sales and give-away aid terms. Giving Sharon the green light, Haig stated on May 27 that: "The time has come to take concerted action in support of both Lebanon's territorial integrity within its internationally recognized borders and a strong central government capable of promoting a free, open, democratic and traditionally pluralistic society."[14]

The time was ripe. Israel massed troops on its northern border and waited for the pretext to invade. By the time Haig was to resign amid the tension rose between his anti-Soviet goals and other U.S. interests in maintaining good relations with the Arab nations, Israel already was on the outskirts of West Beirut.

ANTI-WAR PROTESTS DURING WARTIME

In general, the protests against the war came from several different sources. There were those who condemned the invasion for moral reasons.

---

13. *Jerusalem Post*, April 7, 1981. Though Sharon is long gone from the scene, the rightwing Israeli governments that succeeded him have clearly extended this theory of Israeli regional hegemony, building deep ties to the conservative American "Christian Zionist" movement (as a counterweight to the predominantly liberal American Jewish community) and positing Iran and its proxies as the "axis of evil" to be confronted.
14. *New York Times*, May 27, 1982; quoted in Sheila Ryan, "Israel's Invasion of Lebanon: Background to the Crisis," *Journal of Palestine Studies*, Summer/Fall 1982, p. 36.

Others included a pragmatic critique of Begin and Sharon's strategy, and suggested alternatives ranging from ambiguous calls for negotiations to solve the Palestinian problem to demands for an immediate withdrawal and the establishment of a Palestinian state. Everyone agreed that there was no military solution to the Palestinian problem. As the war's progress quickly exceeded the government's stated goals, criticism also came from more mainstream sources like Labor leaders, and particularly focused on opposition to the invasion of Beirut.

The most painful and angry outpourings came from soldiers returning from the battlefields. Aside from embodying the moral and political criticisms mentioned above, these soldiers felt betrayed by their commanders, in particular by Sharon. Accusing him of lying to the army and the public about the war's purposes and using them as pawns in his plan to restructure the region, they called for his immediate resignation. Some soldiers even refused to serve in Lebanon and went to jail, and a large number of soldiers returning from the war requested not to be sent back. The first and most important point to make about all of these protests, from the mildest to the most radical, was that they were unprecedented in Israel. Never before had public criticism of the government surfaced during wartime.

Peace Now did not react immediately to the invasion for several reasons. One was simply that several of its leaders had been called into the reserves, and the remainder were hesitant to make a major decision without their participation. They were not organizationally prepared for such a case, and in the war's first days many were probably too preoccupied worrying about the safety of family members to react quickly. In addition, the judgement of Peace Now activists involved in the fighting was mixed over whether the movement should hold an immediate demonstration. Thus, it was difficult for the movement's leaders to reach a quick consensus.[15]

A second delaying factor was psychological in nature. Tami Tzarfati, an experienced activist in Tel Aviv, explained to me that summer that Israelis had "a mental problem inhibiting their ability to oppose this war. We were educated that if there's a war, we all go. It's very hard to understand in one

---

15. Author interviews with Shaul Markowitz, August 3, 1982, Rafi Greenberg, August 2, 1982, and Tami Tzarfati, August 10, 1982.

day that it's not that kind of a war." Another activist and social worker in Jerusalem, Ita Gibson, described the "myths" or universally accepted and unquestioned tenets of Israeli politics that act to inhibit public criticism during wartime as "trusting the government, that we know who our enemies are, that wars are justified, that our soldiers are our heroes, [and the] holy myth of consensus—the unity of the country."[16] Thus, during wartime there exists a powerful dynamic toward national solidarity that had been conditioned by what Israelis have seen as five wars of national defense. Criticism was seen as a luxury to be enjoyed only after the nation's security was assured.

This dynamic continued to exert influence on public opinion during the war, from the beginning when opposition leader Yitzhak Rabin called on Israelis to rally behind the government, to later when many Israelis opposed public criticism primarily because they felt it damaged morale in the army and should not be expressed while the lives of Israeli soldiers were at stake. The response of many an Israeli dove was, as a member of Kibbutz Adamit said to me as we sat in a van together on the way to Peace Now's first demonstration against the invasion of Lebanon: "If not now, when? If we wait until after the war has ended, it will be too late to prevent all this unnecessary suffering. It is forbidden to be silent."

For the most part, Peace Now restrained itself for tactical, not psychological or organizational reasons. As spokesman Tzali Reshef later commented, "We were not in favor of the war—not even 40 kilometres [a reference to Begin's stated goal of pushing the PLO out of shelling range of Israel's northern border] ... but we always consider how to carry the maximum public opinion with us."[17] This tactical emphasis on creating broad consensus instead of, as many Peace Now activists tend to put it," being right, but being alone," was long standard operating procedure for the movement. As it turned out, the newer Peace Now branch in Tel Aviv pushed for quicker expressions of protest, for as Tami Tzarfati put it, "we felt that if we feel this way, then everyone must. [The older and more estab-

---

16. Author interview with Ita Gibson, July 20, 1982.
17. *Jerusalem Post International Edition*, March 6-12, 1983, p. 12.

lished] Jerusalem [branch] was more worried about not alienating 'our public'."[18] In the end the more cautious approach won out.

Peace Now's first public protest against the war came in the form of an ad published in the Israeli press on the ninth day of fighting. It read as follows:

> "In this war, the Israeli Army is proving once again that Israel is powerful and self-confident. In this war, we are losing brothers, sons, and friends. In this war, thousands are being uprooted from their homes, and towns are being destroyed. Thousands of civilians are being killed.
>
> What are we getting killed for? What are we killing for? Has there been a national consensus for going into this war? Has there been an immediate threat to our existence? Will it get us out of the cycle of violence, suffering and hatred?
>
> We call upon the Government of Israel: Stop! Now is the time to invite the Palestinian people to join in negotiations for peace. Now is the time for a comprehensive peace based on mutual recognition."[19]

It is worth noting that while severely criticizing the war, the Peace Now ad did not call for an immediate withdrawal from Lebanon—a stand that might have been a more principled but probably less potent politically. Peace Now's decision to postpone an anti-war demonstration while the fighting continued was another tactical compromise the movement made. In the absence of the focus for protest usually provided by the movement, other groups and individuals more radical and less beholden to their "public image" filled the ensuing vacuum.

There were small demonstrations against the war from its very beginning. Several hundred prominent academics and intellectuals called on Israel to stop the fighting and leave Lebanon on June 11.[20] At a press conference on June 22, Professor Yeshayahu Leibowitz–a leading opponent of the occupation–called on soldiers to refuse to serve in Lebanon. And on June 25, some ten to twenty thousand people came to a protest demonstra-

---

18. Author interview with Tami Tzarfati, August 10, 1982.
19. Quoted in Amos Oz, "Has Israel Altered Its Visions?" *The New York Times Magazine*, July 11, 1982, p. 26.
20. *Village Voice*, June 22, 1982.

tion organized by the Ad-hoc Committee Against the War in Lebanon, a group of individuals for the most part affiliated with the Sheli party, the Committee in Solidarity with Bir Zeit University and Peace Now.

Though it seemed that many of the people at this demonstration were wary of participating in a protest while the fighting was continuing, they felt they had no choice. But such was the taboo against protesting while a war was underway that one kibbutznik told me, on our way to the rally, that she was terrified that there would only be a few hundred people there and that the public would turn on them. When we arrived and saw a crowd of 20,000, the relief on her face was palpable. One Peace Now activist at this rally, Shaul Markowitz, told me later that, "Most of the people there were Peace Now people. They had wanted to express their feelings against the war and [since] Peace Now hadn't [organized a demonstration]," they went to a more radical demonstration. In any case, Peace Now had by then decided to hold an anti-war demonstration the following week.[21] Its restraint was vindicated, for this rally succeeded in gathering 100,000 people in Tel Aviv—as many as had previously turned out for Peace Now's biggest rally on the eve of Camp David.

Ads for that rally repeated Peace Now's earlier call for a historic compromise with the Palestinians and also included a demand for Ariel Sharon's resignation. Attacking his use of "lies and deceptions" to pull the country into the war, Peace Now angrily denounced the use of the army for imperialistic purposes, saying: "We were called to fight for the security of the Galilee but we found ourselves fighting in order to eliminate the Palestinian problem by force of arms; to do the Phalangists' job for them; to further the cause of annexation on the West Bank ... Never another war like this one."[22]

This new phenomenon of protest during wartime did not go unnoticed by Israel's leaders, especially because it did not focus on the traditional themes of post-war criticism. As the Argentine-Jewish journalist Jacobo Timerman wrote in his eloquent antiwar memoir *The Longest War*: "In the Lebanon war the familiar pattern was broken, and Begin perceived this at

---

21. Author interview with Shaul Markowitz, August 3, 1982.
22. Peace Now leaflet, July 1982.

once. For the first time Israelis were thinking about what they had done to another people. They were feeling guilt, even shame."[23]

A battle to maintain the public's belief in the legitimacy of the war then began—a battle fought in the press and in the streets. Begin and Sharon added lies and distortions on top of each other, in order to maintain the "big lie"—that this was a necessary war of national self-defense. And every step of the way, brave voices rose in opposition to this lie.

Sharon claimed that Israel had lost 1,392 victims to Palestinian terrorism over the previous fifteen years. According to journalist Baruch Leshem, police reports showed the correct number to be 282. He found that Sharon had greatly expanded this number by including other categories of victims not at all relevant to his claim.[24] In a similar manner, Israel attempted to prove that captured PLO weapons caches could have provided enough arms for "a million men." These weapons were publicly displayed in Tel Aviv and used as well in Israel's propaganda effort abroad. Labor M.K. Yossi Sarid charged the government with gross exaggeration and backing him up was Ha'aretz's respected military correspondent, Ze'ev Schiff. He wrote: "There are indeed many [captured] weapons, but there is no foundation that there is enough to fully equip five divisions—perhaps there is enough equipment to equip one division ... Did these arms threaten Israel's existence? They did constitute a danger of raids, shelling and terror, but in no sense a danger to our existence. The strength of an infantry division with partial support is no danger to Israeli existence, unless we suddenly desire to ignore the strength of the I.D.F."[25]

Begin, as was his nature, returned to the Holocaust as his justification for the inviolability of Jewish survival and his willingness to use any means to preserve that survival. Likening Arafat and his men to the Nazis, he asked rhetorically, "If Hitler was hiding in a building with twenty innocent people, wouldn't you bomb the building?" And, "if even if Arafat recognized us, we would not recognize him. Hitler didn't recognize us."[26]

For Begin, Beirut 1982 became Berlin 1945, the PLO guerrillas the Nazi armies, and the Palestinians themselves the Germans. The war was his

---

23. Jacobo Timerman, *The Longest War*, pp. 34-35.
24. *Ha'aretz*, July 16, 1982.
25. *Jerusalem Post*, July 13, 1982; *Ha'aretz*, July 18, 1982.
26. *Ha'aretz*, June 21, 1982; *Al Ha'mishmar*, July 14, 1982.

revenge, the Jewish people's revenge against their oppressors and would-be oppressors. Regarding world-wide criticism of Israel's invasion, he would say, in effect, "the world's always been against the Jews." He and others like him used these analogies and reasoning to whip up Israeli hostility to the Palestinians, who were seen and always referred to as "terrorists," never "fighters" or "guerrillas" or even "civilians" when such was the case.

The existence of an enemy is always part of the emotional and philosophical underpinning of nationalism, and that the first step in any nation's war against another people is the dehumanization of that group. For Americans, the Japanese became "Japs," the Vietnamese "gooks." For Germans the Jews became "vermin, scum." And for Begin's Israel, and before him Golda Meir's Israel, the Palestinians became "terrorists, two-legged animals," which Begin and Meir wished did not exist. "Gooks" one may kill because they have less respect for human life, "vermin" one stamps out, and "terrorists" one liquidates. Many Israelis sneered at the suggestion that Arafat was a "moderate."

The shame at this willful manipulation of the Holocaust to justify the war in Lebanon and many painful parallels between the Nazi treatment of the Jews and Israel's treatment of the Palestinians went very deep for some Israelis. The Association of Anti-Nazi Fighters and Victims of Nazism in Israel issued a statement, saying in part: "We who came out of the Nazi inferno, humiliated, oppressed, bereaved for our close ones ... we who knew how to share our fate with members of other nations and to depend on each other for rescue; we who saw in the state of Israel the fulfillment of historic justice to our nation after the horrors of the Holocaust ... are ashamed of you, Menachem Begin, and of your racist notions about the Palestinian Arab people."[27]

There are two possible and divergent lessons to be learned from the Holocaust: the progressive response of "never again shall any people be victimized" and the narrower realpolitik response of "never again will this happen to us." Many Israelis perhaps thought they could have it both ways, a nation-state that was also "a light unto the nations."

---

27. Quoted in Ellen Cantarow, "Eternal War—Darkness Descends on a Light Unto Nations," *Mother Jones*, December 1982, p. 29.

"We must never do to others what others did to us," they said, and convinced of their own righteousness, came to speak of Israel's occupation of the West Bank and Gaza as the most "liberal" in the world. In a paradoxical sense, some good could have come from Begin's sacrilegious use of the Holocaust, for in removing all remaining pretensions to the moral self-righteousness that prevented so many from seeing themselves as oppressors, he opened a path to the needed national self-searching on the Palestinian question. But in the short run, Begin's rhetoric had the intended effect. According to the *Jerusalem Post*, 93% of the population supported the invasion one month after it began.[28] Yet, two weeks later, another poll found that two-thirds of the public opposed the armed seizure of West Beirut, the PLO's last stronghold.[29]

Perhaps the most significant opposition to surface during the war came from soldiers themselves. At first their protests were personal, spontaneous acts of self-purification. As one veteran of ten years in the paratroops said, "One gets the mobilization order, and does the best job one can. But then one returns from the war, and one doesn't feel discharged. One has the moral duty to tell the truth about what happened."[30] Groups of soldiers sent many collective letters to newspapers, complaining of Sharon's cynical use of their loyalty, demanding his resignation, demanding an accounting.

The soldiers' protests eventually coalesced around two new groups. The first called itself "Soldiers Against Silence" ("Hayalim Neged Shtika"). Their protest grew primarily out of what they saw as the army's cynical use for political goals, the fact that it was an avoidable war, and that they had been lied to. Peace Now activist Shaul Markowitz spoke of friends of his in Soldiers Against Silence who had been given orders at the war's outset to advance towards and engage Syrian forces. Men spoke of hearing cease-fires declared on the radio while they were being ordered to start hostilities. Soldiers took to listening to the Lebanese radio to get a more accurate description of the war's development.

Disillusionment was rampant on the front; according to the *Jerusalem*

---

28. *Jerusalem Post*, July 4, 1982.
29. Timerman, op.cit., p. 80.
30. Ibid., p . 69.

Post's Hirsh Goodman, who wrote, "Three Israeli military correspondents were surrounded by officers and men of four top fighting units, who accused them of covering up the truth, of lying to the public, of not reporting on the real mood at the front and of being lackeys of the defense minister. We were accused by the overwhelming majority of men— including senior officers—of allowing this war to grow out of all proportion to the original goals, by mindlessly repeating official explanations we all knew to be false."[31] Soldiers Against Silence quickly gathered the signatures of hundreds of reservists who wanted an end to the fighting, opposed any entry into West Beirut, and called for Sharon's resignation and inquiry into the government's handling of the war.[32]

The second group, Yesh Gvul ("There is a Limit"), was more radical than Soldiers Against Silence in two ways. It had no qualms calling for an immediate withdrawal from Lebanon, in addition to attacking the government for all the same reasons as Soldiers Against Silence. But most importantly, Yesh Gvul announced that its members did not necessarily accept military discipline. With respect to the question of resisting service in Lebanon, its members replied that they neither accepted nor rejected it— that it was up to each soldier to decide for himself.[33] Prior to this, Israel had almost no tradition of pacifism or of conscientious objection. For the men who began to contemplate it seriously, and for the several who actually refused service and went to jail, it was a very painful question. As paratrooper Alon Shemi told *New York Times* correspondent David Shipler, "[The army represents] the widest Zionist consensus of the people who live here: our loyalty, our responsibility for the army, our willingness to fight. [It has always been based on our complete confidence] that the army would be used just for necessity, for what we call no-choice wars. [By refusing to fight] you break the basic agreement of collective life in this country."[34]

One soldier, who admitted that, despite his opposition to Begin, Sharon and the war, he would return to the front if ordered to do so, said, "If I

---

31. Ibid., p. 23.
32. Author interview with Shaul Markowitz, August 3, 1982.
33. *Al Ha'Mishmar*, July 14, 1982.
34. David K. Shipler, "Israel: Voices of Moral Anguish," *New York Times Magazine*, February 27, 1983, p. 65.

break the rules, I break myself." Yet many men spoke of an ambiguous "red line" that they would not cross, and nearly all described their growing alienation from the majority of Israeli society that did not share their concerns. Said Shemi: "I can't see myself now taking part in a war, a mission, that would be clearly to achieve political aims that don't have to do with our basic existence here. I might find myself unable to live here. In the streets I feel like a stranger."[35]

By making a war lacking a national consensus behind it, Begin and Sharon unwittingly started the slow erosion of the army's solidarity. The doubts and "grave misgivings" that the authors of the Officers' Letter had referred to four years earlier were being realized. The example set by Colonel Eli Geva, who resigned his command and offered to serve as an ordinary soldier rather than lead the invasion of West Beirut, was very important, for it provided an alternative example for the future, for Israelis who might otherwise say "I was only following orders."

Despite all these protests, even the 100,000 massed by Peace Now, the government retained the support of a large majority of the public. To buttress its majority in the Knesset, and as if to signal its real intentions, the Begin government absorbed the right-wing annexationist Tehiya party into its governing coalition in late July. The head of Tehiya, Professor Yuval Ne'eman, spoke of southern Lebanon as Israeli territory, and in early August the newspapers reported that the army's chief rabbi was distributing a Hebraicized map of Lebanon, on which the country was marked as the territory that was once occupied by the ancient Jewish tribe of Asher.[36] More Palestinian mayors on the West Bank were dismissed during July, and Bir Zeit University was closed again. "We are trapped," read Peace Now's leaflet for its anti-war demonstration and indeed they were. The horrible, sometimes twelve-hour-long, shelling of West Beirut started, and the movement's activists agonized at their inability to stop the bloodshed.

Paradoxically, the success of Peace Now's July 3 anti-war protest served to stymie other major actions. Having proven the depth of the public opposition, what more could they do? Another attempt at a big demonstration would take a lot of work and in any case might fail to increase their influ-

35. Shipler, op.cit., p.66.
36. Timerman, op.cit., pp. 128, 139.

ence, especially if less people came. That August, I attended two meetings of Peace Now's leadership council in Jerusalem where activists debated a range of practical ideas like vigils, petitions and door-to-door leafleting to proposals for small demonstrations in the Galilee, or of rabbinic leaders; from proposals for the compilation of a "White Paper" on the war to demands that Peace Now "oppose the 'fascistization' of Israel."

"What do do and how is the question," Tsali Reshef said at the first of those meetings. He admitted that he was afraid to call for another big demonstration "and flop." Janet Aviad responded that she still wanted to try something with a "big impact...something to mobilize half the country." But no one had the obvious answer. "We don't have soldiers," Reshef noted. "Sometimes we can get a lot of people out. But let's not waste our energy—just to say we are here is not enough."[37]

Movement leaders also worried that despite their intrinsic value, many of these smaller protests would be ignored by the media. Indeed, vigils and protests held regularly by the smaller and more radical anti-war groups tended to get only occasional coverage and more often than not resulted in violent confrontations with gangs of Begin supporters calling them "traitors," "Arafatists" and "Nazis." It was a time of great despair, frustration and radicalization for a significant minority of Israeli society. Every day Israel was bombing Beirut and blowing up the homes of Palestinians in the West Bank and nothing they could imagine doing seemed to matter. The power to end the war rested in the hands of others—others too deluded and opportunistic to see the error of their ways.

Though in the final analysis, Peace Now and the other anti-war groups were obviously unable to stop the war, one might argue that it was their influence, especially from within the army, that prevented Sharon from ordering a bloody frontal assault on West Beirut. But in relation to the core issues of imperial security strategy versus legitimate self-defense, and annexation versus compromise with the Palestinians, the Begin government and a good proportion of Israeli society held firm to the notion that brute force was the only solution. Even so, in the first week of August a poll conducted for the conservative daily *Yediot Aharonot*, found in terms of a solution to the Palestinian problem, 16% of the Israeli public favored the

---

37. Author's contemporaneous notes from August 1, 1982 and August 15, 1982 meetings.

establishment of a Palestinian state, 37% supported their return to Jordan and demilitarization of some of the occupied territories, and 33% favored annexation.[38]

Peace Now remained an extremely important part of the Israeli political scene. One measure of the growth in the power of its ideas was the size of the turnout at the demonstration called by Peace Now and the Labor Party to protest the mid-September massacre of Palestinians in the Sabra and Shatila refugee camps of Beirut. A stunning 400,000 people—10% of Israel's population—demanded and finally got an official government inquiry into Israel's role in the massacre. According to one Labor M.K., "it would have only been a little smaller if Peace Now had organized it alone."[39] The resulting Kahan Commission report eventually forced the ouster of Ariel Sharon from the Defense Ministry, as well as the removal of several other high-ranking military men, for having "indirect responsibility" for allowing the massacre to take place. Sadly, the political turmoil and unrest surrounding the commission's conclusions and the Begin government's slowness in following its recommendations also led to the death in early 1983 of a Peace Now demonstrator, Emil Grunzweig, and the injury of several others by a grenade thrown by right-wing fanatics. The polarization of Israeli society reached a new height with Grunzweig's murder.

A year later, 38 Members of Knesset added their names to a Peace Now event commemorating the first anniversary of his death. This period was the height of the movement's influence. And yet. In January of 1984, I visited Israel again on a short trip where I was able to speak with a number of peace activists. Peace Now's Tzali Reshef was generous with his time. He was wrestling with many issues, from how Israel could extricate itself from Lebanon and resolve ongoing tensions with its neighbor Syria, to the heart of the conflict with the Palestinians and whether more radical groups like Yesh Gvul, who were advocating for civil disobedience by soldiers, could shift the country.

For the most part, he was hopeful. "I think the Lebanon War has taught the Israeli public a very serious lesson, that is, with force alone you cannot solve problems." He also was quite clear about the limits of Peace Now's

---

38. *Yediot Aharonot*, August 16, 1982.
39. *Jerusalem Post International Edition*, March 6-12, 1983, p. 12.

influence. "Reality is much stronger than our demonstrations," he noted warily. "The tragic thing about Peace Now is that it is more powerful and influential when catastrophes occur. It's more difficult today to call a demonstration of 100,000 people that it was in the third week of the war. People get used to everything and people feel tired." On the other hand, he credited that July 3, 1982 mass rally with having prevented Begin and Sharon from fully invading West Beirut.

He also offered a realistic appraisal of the movement's power. "One should make clear. We don't believe that we are able to stop settlements. We can only raise public opinion against them, so that the established political structure will be influenced and change." As for Yesh Gvul's embrace of refusing to serve in Lebanon or the occupied territories, he said, "Today, to refuse on the basis of your political views is to break the very basis of our society. And it is legitimizing the behavior of the settlers."[40]

Andre Draznin, a leader of Yesh Gvul who I also interviewed that January in Israel, vehemently disagreed. "It's a lie to say that Gush Emunim activists need Yesh Gvul to legitimate their breach of the law. They have been breaking the law systematically since 1968." He added that people who criticized "refuseniks" like him "ignore the reality of our developing situation...which is that we, peace activists, have no power at all to seriously change the development of events. If we don't use more radical weapons, such as civil disobedience, there will never come a situation where a fight against Gush Emunim will take place. If not, the situation will become more and more stable and we will lose the fight. It will be the death of the peace camp and the death for the chances of Israeli-Palestinian coexistence."

He added, darkly:

"Being a good boy, doing all the things that you say shouldn't be done, it changes you. After a year, two or three years, when you bombard Beirut, kill civilians, when you become an integral part of the occupation. You come somehow to legitimatize the occupation—to develop post-facto justifi-

---

40. Author interview with Tzali Reshef, January 1983.

cations for it. That is, the situation changes you if you don't forcefully oppose it."[41]

ISRAEL'S TURNING POINT

Looking back at the 1977-1983 period in Israel's history with the benefit of hindsight, it seems clear that this is when the foundation stones for today's intractable conflict were laid, if not cemented. While the Begin-Sharon government did not last, it vastly strengthened the settlement movement in the West Bank, most notably by allowing radical settlers to take over buildings in the heart of Hebron. And while Sharon's adventure in Lebanon ultimately failed, it taught future rightwing governments the necessity of building more political support in America for Israeli expansionism. And most important for Israeli society, it marked the beginning of its fracturing across class and ethnic lines, as diverging views on how to address the Palestinian problem cleaved Israelis against each other.

With respect to the Palestinian question, the policies of Begin and Sharon, coupled with the historic legacy of the Labor establishment, clearly polarized the Israeli public. While Begin supposedly recognized Palestinian "legitimate rights" at Camp David and promised them "full autonomy," in reality, he opted for what journalist Danny Rubenstein called "deluxe annexation," that is, unrestricted Jewish settlement and the full integration of the economies of Israel and the occupied territories. No longer seen as bargaining chips for a peace deal, the territories began to serve not only "as a protected market for Israeli goods, but also a source of cheap labor for Israel's economy." All this Israel gets without extending the benefits of the Israeli social welfare system to the Palestinians, and, more importantly, without extending them even limited autonomy (let alone self-rule or equal rights).[42] For good reason, critics began to refer to this status quo as an Israeli form of apartheid—a conclusion that has only gained salience with time.

Begin's approach to Palestinian nationalism was also shown in starker

---

41. Author interview with Andre Draznin, January 1983. See also Sifry, op. cit, *The Progressive*, August 1984.
42. Danny Rubenstein, "Deluxe Annexation," *New Outlook*, June 1981; *Jerusalem Post*, May 9, 1978.

relief by the attempt to eradicate or cripple it in the 1982 war in Lebanon. In addition, some observers noted that Israel apparently had concealed imperial economic objectives in that war—most notably a desire to disrupt the economy of southern Lebanon and link it to Israel's economy (along with the water resources of the Litani river). In reaction, some Israelis even began to speak of a "North Bank." With respect to the dominant tradition in Zionism of "creating facts on the ground," Begin's way is new only in one respect—his delusion that Israel had the power, internal as well as external, to impose its will on the region and on the Palestinians. Though other Israeli governments may have sought similar goals, they never initiated an imperial war to achieve them. There is a fundamental difference between demanding "secure, defensible borders" in exchange for territorial withdrawal and insisting on the whole "Land of Israel."

From this period, two paths emerged for Israel. One is the path of fantasy, Begin's way (and now Netanyahu's way), a pathological worship of land and intoxication with the possibilities of military superiority, a way that ignores the realities of the international situation and of Israel's economic vulnerabilities, a way that denies and seeks to exterminate Palestinian nationalism. The other is the path of realism.[43]

The realist position has several components. In certain ways, it corresponds with the dovish arguments that go back to the beginning of Zionism. For one, it recognizes that given demographic trends, annexation of the West Bank and Gaza will mean an eventual non-Jewish majority in Israel. Realists give little weight to the so-called Zionist faith in a new burst of Jewish immigration.

A second aspect of the realist position, voiced for example by Begin's former intelligence advisor Yehoshafat Harkabi, is the acceptance that "the central norm of our period is that of self-determination for recognized communities. The attempt to obstruct the self-determination of such a community is an anachronism that cannot last long."[44] Thus, as early as the late 1970s, realists were ready to admit that the Labor Party's anti-PLO "Jordanian option"—withdrawal along the lines of the Allon plan (which

---

43. These two terms come from Yehoshafat Harkabi's 1982 book, *The Bar Kokhba Syndrome: Risk and Realism in International Politics.*
44. *Ma'ariv*, May 10, 1978.

calls for annexing most of the occupied territories' arable land and natural resources)—was dead in the face of Palestinian nationalism.

Though Begin may have believed that Israel could have its cake and eat it too—that it could hold the West Bank and Gaza (and possibly southern Lebanon as well), profit from its neo-colonialist exploitation of these sources of cheap labor, water, and captive markets, and maintain full U.S. support—others were not as sure. They argued that Israeli adventurism in Lebanon could undermine the Egyptian-Israeli peace treaty, and pointed as well to the American desire for a pro-U.S. alliance of the conservative Arab states of Egypt, Jordan, and Saudi Arabia, which would entail greater pressure on Israel to give in on the Palestinian question.

Indeed, it was during these turning point years that, faced with these long-term trends, some Israeli strategists, arguing from a realpolitik position, came out in favor of Israeli initiatives that, instead of attempting to eliminate or bypass the PLO, favored direct negotiations with them toward the establishment of a Palestinian state in the West Bank and the Gaza Strip. Such an argument was made by Mark A. Heller, in his 1983 book, *A Palestinian State: The Implications for Israel.* He suggested that such a settlement—consisting of a peace treaty between Israel and the PLO (or any other authoritative spokesman of the Palestinian national movement) that would be ratified by the critical Arab states, and that would be based on the 1949 armistice lines (with possible minor rectifications and a special regime for Jerusalem) and the Palestinian acceptance of verifiable restrictions on force levels, equipment and deployment—would be the best of all evils.[45]

Cognizant of the other aspects of the realist position, Heller advocated a direct settlement with the PLO because he saw any solution that circumvented them as less durable and more vulnerable to PLO-inspired destabilization. Since he recognized that it was in Israel's security interest to induce the Palestinians' "sole representative" to legitimize such a historic compromise between the two nations, he opposed any solution that would "relieve the PLO of the necessity to purge itself of its absolutist ideology, its maximalist goals, and its extremist factions. In addition, he noted that a direct settlement with the PLO had the best likelihood of securing lasting

---

45. Mark A. Heller, *A Palestinian State: The Implications for Israel,* pp. 5-6.

concessions demanded by Israel with respect to restrictions on Palestinian military capabilities. Lastly, he argued that, given Israel's sensitivity and willingness to take anticipatory actions to preempt perceived threats, continued Palestinian independence would be effectively hostage to internal moderation and non-threatening Arab behavior.[46]

Realists like Harkabi and Heller came to advocate Israeli recognition of Palestinian national aspirations after detailed analyses of the interplay of external strategic factors and the implications of ·the various alternatives, particularly continuation of the status quo, or Israel's security and its Jewish, democratic character. Starting in 1977 and continuing through the following decades, Peace Now was the primary popular advocate of these ideas in Israel. But it has always been a minority in the country, though a much larger minority than Judah Magnes' Brit Shalom or the Movement for Peace and Security.

---

46. Ibid,, pp. 146-148.

CHAPTER 7
PEACE NOW AS A MOVEMENT ORGANIZATION

IN FIVE TUMULTUOUS YEARS, Peace Now grew from a small group of angry young men to a mass movement with over two thousand core activists and hundreds of thousands of supporters out of a country of four million. During those years, its cautious strategy of speaking in terms of Israel's interests and focusing on broad principles that ought to govern official policy made it by the summer of 1982, as Janet Aviad said, "the major peace group to which the government relates in every one of its attacks."[1] Peace Now's existence and success in mobilizing large segments of the Israeli public served to legitimize dissent within the Zionist framework on fundamental questions pertaining to Israel's character and purpose.

Just as Begin's brand of Zionism represented one way of resolving the internal contradictions in Zionism that the Palestinian issue and the territorial issue raise, Peace Now represented another way. Begin's way was the use of force to solve disputes. Peace Now's was compromise and negotiations. Begin's way sought to strip the Palestinian of his basic dignity, while Peace Now recognized that the desire for Jewish or Palestinian national self-determination comes from the same human source. Begin's way took Jews away from their tradition of justice and made them into oppressors, while Peace Now sought that Jews return to the human family by learning

---

1. Author interview with Janet Aviad, August 3, 1982.

to live in peace with their neighbors. Most importantly, though Begin tried to portray his actions as being in Israel's national interest, Peace Now made a powerful case for the recognition of Palestinian national rights on not only moral grounds, but in terms of Israel's self-interest. These differences remain relevant today.

How did Peace Now go about this work? Throughout its early years, Peace Now adamantly maintained a quasi-anarchist internal structure. It had no formal leaders, no central office, no formal membership, no paid officials. These only came much later. Local branches would have bi-weekly open meetings, and people who wanted to get more heavily involved were invited to participate on standing committees that dealt with on-going activities like finance, demonstrations, publicity, literature, local outreach, youth groups, lobbying and the media. Each branch chose a few representatives to the movement's central forum, where matters of major policy were debated and decided. At each level of decision, the movement operated by consensus, which meant that any sizable minority had a built-in veto, and no one person could take unilateral initiatives.

The guiding principle for the movement's organization was volun-teerism. One representative critic of tendencies toward bureaucratization and the establishment of paying positions within the movement was Roni Siegel. "I believe in people giving and doing because they believe in it," he told me. In his opinion, paid activists and more structure would skew activities to fit the structure, rather than keep the movement fluid and responsive to external developments.[2] Volunteerism does have its costs, unfortunately. One is the burden that it places on the core of activists who keep the movement running from day to day. "Last time [i.e. Peace Now from 1978-1980], people burned themselves out," Janet Aviad said in the summer of 1982. When, as was the case the first time around, the move-ment's lack of formal structure led to the formation of an ad-hoc group of real decision-makers, this problem was compounded by the lack of other people who could fill in and keep the movement going. As we have seen, part of the reason Peace Now became moribund in the fall of 1980 was that the small group began to lose its internal harmony and balance, key people left, and others could not fill their places.

---

2. Author interview with Roni Siegel, August 2, 1982.

The second generation of Peace Now's leadership was aware of these problems and consciously sought to prevent their recurrence. For one, the movement's second act was no longer run by a more-or-less closed clique of men in their early thirties and late twenties. An older generation had a more influential role and gave the movement some stability and continuity. Yet the structure remained open and supportive. "In order that activists don't get too tired, people switch in and out. [That we have had] enough people to do this is a very healthy sign," said Aviad.

At the same time, she said, the movement was constantly absorbing new blood. "We spot the new people at meetings now and invite them to the middle level forum, and 'test' them to see if they're serious by giving them a job to do," Aviad told me.[3] One activist new to the movement during this time, Shaul Markowitz, remarked that he originally had thought that Peace Now was run by a small group of self-appointed leaders. Then he saw the suggestion of another new activist, a friend of his, to take on the controversial action at Telem in March 1982 become a reality. "I was really happy to find that the criticism of the leadership wasn't true," he reflected. "People who attack the lack of democracy in the movement are just not really involved. If they want, they can be active and involved in decisions as they want."[4]

Still, as is true for all movements, volunteerism and the lack of structure inevitably causes problems that only experience and experimentation can solve. Sometimes it meant that, for unforeseen personal circumstances, a job got delayed or didn't get done. And it still left time-consuming burdens like paperwork on key activists whose time and experience was invaluable. Said Aviad back then, "I think if we want to become a bigger or more serious movement, certain things have to be taken off the shoulders of those most involved."[5] In a new branch like Tel Aviv, there was the problem that while 250 people came regularly to the general meetings, fifteen core people ended up doing all the work. As Tami Tzarfati said, "When it's 250 people we don't really get to know them."[6] More efficient

---

3. Author interview with Janet Aviad, August 3, 1982.
4. Author interview with Shaul Markowitz, August 3, 1982.
5. Author interview with Janet Aviad, August 3, 1982.
6. Author interview with Tami Tzarfati, August 10, 1982.

ways of integrating and training new activists were needed–a challenge every movement centered on volunteer activism faces.

A broader series of questions dealt with the topic of tactics. For Peace Now activists, the message in favor of compromise and reconciliation was clear. The question was how to express it effectively—that is, so that another person would be convinced or made to think, so that public opinion would change, so that Members of Knesset would vote differently, and so that government policy and ideology would change. The movement faced several difficult obstacles: the scarcity of open forums for the exchange and spreading of ideas, the fact that many people lacked the luxury of having free time to spend working for Peace Now, the complacency of many Peace Now supporters (particularly among people living on the kibbutzim), the impermeability of the Knesset and political parties to American-style lobbying efforts, the social gap between Ashkenazim and Sephardim, and the volatile and unpredictable nature of Israeli politics. In its early years, Peace Now tried to tackle all of these problems at the same time, with mixed results.

Peace Now's tactics then could be broken down between short-term, massive public actions and ongoing, quiet outreach to groups and individuals. With reference to the former, the movement showed itself to be remarkably adept at mobilizing the "already convinced." Between the phone networks of the major city branches and the kibbutzim, it was able to gather over 3,000 people on short notice. When a major demonstration was called, tens of thousands of people showed up or sometimes more. But experienced activists noted some problems.

For example, because many committed supporters had demanding jobs and careers, there were limitations on their willingness to sacrifice. As Roni Siegel explained to me, "It's not meant to be a revolutionary group that dominates your whole life-style. Most of the members have full-time jobs and devote their spare time to Peace Now."[7] Few Israelis, even college students, felt that they have the economic freedom to devote their time to activism. And, as Moti Perry complained, "Kibbutzniks are even more reluctant." For example, he told me, "We wanted a kibbutz a day to sit-in in order to close Eilon Moreh permanently [January 1980]. But we knew our

---

7. Author interview with Roni Siegel, August 2, 1982.

people, [and that therefore] we could only hold it for two or three days. So we looked for a plausible excuse to stop it ... before people started going home."[8]

And so, in that case, in exchange for getting the great publicity of having non-violently closed Eilon Moreh, the movement ended the protest for the minor concession of a meeting with Defense Minister Weizman. Several movement activists expressed frustration at the complacency of many kibbutzniks. "All of these people sit in front of their T.V.'s crying," said Perry. Tami Tzarfati, a former kibbutznik like him, was more understanding. "They don't feel the acuteness of it, except in a war. They are isolated and happy and out of touch ... They don't feel that if you have a Peace Now sticker on your car people will spit on you and you might get hit. I am more troubled when I send my children to school and on Tu'B'shvat [Arbor Day] they go to plant trees at a settlement on the West Bank."[9]

Indeed, with the benefit of hindsight, it is clear that many Peace Now activists never made the same intense commitment to their cause that rightwing Jewish settlers made to theirs. Seizing land illegally and then holding it until receiving the blessing of the government required a high level of zeal, which for many settlers came from the combination of religious and nationalist fervor. Peace Now, by contrast, relied heavily on bringing out large crowds at demonstrations meant to show that public opinion was on their side. Though it took frequent actions to protest illegal settlements, it never evolved a sustained way of forcing the government to choose between backing settlements versus dismantling to maintain the possibility of a path to peace. As the old saying goes, an organized minority can be much stronger than a disorganized majority.

Mordecai Bar-On, one of the movement's elders, acknowledged this weakness in his 1996 book, *In Pursuit of Peace*. In it, he wrote:

"By their very nature, Peace Now activities were transient phenomena, whereas Gush Emunim created permanent facts on the ground. With regard to the settlements, Peace Now advocated a negative policy of what not to

8. Author interview with Moti Perry, January-February 1983.
9. Author interview with Tami Tzafarti, August 10, 1982.

do, whereas Gush Emunim undertook positive activities and created new concrete realities. Members of Gush Emunim were engaged in a project that involved their entire lives. Their objective was not a temporary protest but a total commitment to an ideology of divine redemption that called upon them to change the reality in and on the land in Judea and Samaria. In contrast, members of Peace Now, by the very nature of their purpose, came and went depending on the issue and environment of the moment, and at the end of the day they all returned home. Hence, in terms of the personal conviction and commitment of its members, Peace Now was the weaker party."[10]

Peace Now activists noted several other problems with relying on demonstrations. For one, the actual logistics and preparations sapped time and volunteers away from long-term efforts—though of course a big demonstration had a clearer and more immediate payoff than hundreds of living-room meetings. There was also the danger that by overusing the tactic of rallies, without achieving tangible results, the movement might also be causing people to lose heart and become disillusioned. This seems to be what occurred during the movement's drawn-out, losing battle against the settlements in the West Bank. Lastly, some came to worry that demonstrations simply gave people a chance to "wash their consciences" by showing up, and then doing nothing further.[11]

It takes a relatively low level of commitment to attend a rally, as opposed to organizing a local meeting or distributing leaflets, for example. Yet for many Israelis, attendance at a Peace Now demonstration was a major step. It remained the organizers' problem how to get them to be more involved. As it is, mass demonstrations remain a very important and effective means of affecting public opinion and influencing the government. And, as Mordecai Bar-On commented, "We have to ask ourselves: what will happen if there are no protests?"[12]

In terms of longer-term efforts to reach out to and influence the general public, Peace Now activists tried several approaches—all with varying

---

10. Mordecai Bar-On, *In Pursuit of Peace* (Washington, DC: US Institute of Peace, 1996), p. 111.
11. Author interview with Dedi Zucker, August 18, 1982.
12. *Jerusalem Post International Edition*, March 6-12, 1983, p. 13.

degrees of effectiveness. Generally, they relied on the Israeli media, and especially the press, to help spread its message. Very often, the movement's smaller actions and rallies were specifically oriented toward getting press coverage. "[Suggestions] have to be measured against effectiveness," said Aviad. "Where can you do something where you will make a big, big impact?"[13] Paradoxically, they found that as their ability to stage small and frequent demonstrations grew, the media's interest in them declined—a dilemma that has stymied peace movements the world over. As Rafi Greenberg commented to me, "To get press now, we have to invent something new."[14]

The movement's activists also recognized that they had to find more ways to take their message directly to the "unconverted." Public forums usually amounted to little more than preaching to the choir. Regular neighborhood meetings in people's homes were also seen as "coffee klatches" rather than real persuasion sessions. Many Peace Now organizers told me that these provided the least tangible impact for the greatest amount of work. However, neighborhood meetings remained a valuable tool depending on the degree to which they were used to recruit, train, and build a nuclei of activists in areas where support for Peace Now was weak —particularly in Sephardi neighborhoods where an Ashkenazi outsider from Peace Now was usually unwelcome.

Another important route to the unconverted was through public high schools, an available open forum in a country that lacks many. High schools regularly invite speakers from various political viewpoints. "We think it is very important," said Tzarfati. "The high schools now are very right-wing and a lot of students don't really care."[15] Youth groups organized by Peace Now activists also tried to make inroads in the high schools. But what the movement really needed in order to fully exploit this potential was a cadre of full-time, paid speakers who could travel around the country visiting schools and community centers. Unfortunately, the idea of paid organizers, even for this limited but vital task, was anathema for Peace Now in its early years.

---

13. Author interview with Janet Aviad, August 3, 1982.
14. Author interview with Rafi Greenberg, August 2, 1982..
15. Author interview with Tami Tzarfati, August 10, 1982.

The movement also often used the tactic of tabling in public places to disseminate literature, expand its telephone network, gather signatures on petitions, raise money, and increase its public visibility. From the very beginning, this approach was often very effective, but sometimes risky. A small minority of the Israeli public, but a violent and extreme one, hated Peace Now and the peace movement and all it stood for. These are people who refused to listen or discuss—they had made an emotional judgment. Some observers saw the emergence of this faction as part of a "fascist" process occurring in Israel. When anti-dove violence is combined with viciously racist attacks on Arabs—as has occurred many times on Israel's campuses and in the streets—one rightfully began to worry. What was most disturbing is the union of religious intolerance and fundamentalism with ultra-nationalism and the willingness to use violence against one's ideological adversary.

Shaul Markowitz described what this was like for him. "I remember one day I was sitting at a public table with Yiftach—he was one of the first officers who signed the letter. He is handicapped—his hand was burned in the Yom Kippur war and he also received a medal then. Some people were coming down the street, saying 'I'm sure you didn't serve in the army,' 'You traitor—I'll kill you,' and other unpleasant things ... You could feel some people really hate you."

He reflected that he didn't know "which way Israel was going," adding, "One week after the [Lebanon] war began, there was a small demonstration by the Prime Minister's Office ... Eight returned soldiers, and the wife of one, and the father of someone who was killed in the war... And two busloads of people came from a pro-government rally, and they beat them really hard ... Such things drive me crazy ... something is twisted here, when soldiers are called traitors."

He recalled a science-fiction story he read in *Ha'aretz*, "It was about November 1982 ... Israel was still in Lebanon, and someone came back from reserve service, and shot a Peace Now person at a petition table in Tel Aviv ... It's starting to be more and more realistic," he worried."[16] This was from an interview in August 1982. Barely half a year later, in February 1983, right-wing thugs attacked Peace Now people outside the emergency

---

16. Author interview with Shaul Markowitz, August 3, 1982.

room as they rushed demonstrators injured by the grenade attack that killed Emil Grunzweig to the hospital.

Most of the anti-Peace Now violence then was rooted in Begin's popularity among the Sephardim, who linked Peace Now to the Ashkenazi establishment. The movement's attacks on Begin were viewed by some as attacks on the pride of the Sephardim. And, many Sephardim subscribed to Begin's political views as well.

Peace Now made small inroads in the Sephardi community, partially by working with reform groups like the Ohalim anti-poverty movement in Jerusalem. It was a very slow and frustrating process. Yossi Shayit, an activist from Jerusalem, described an early failure:

"You'd think that the people who are on the bottom economically and socially would be interested in peace because it would release resources that would be allocated to them. We sat one evening ... two evenings, for hours and hours trying to write up a little manifesto arguing this point ... We got this thing nicely written up and memorized and rehearsed and everything. And one of our people went to Romena, which is, I guess, a slum in Jerusalem. And the first thing the people said was 'listen, it's about time we had servants, too.' That's what being a hawk means to somebody who's been on the bottom ... those people who've been stepped on forever finally have the Arabs to do the same to ... that pretty much shattered our whole rationale about the link between the economy and peace."[17]

The movement recognized that it had a serious image problem compounding the over-representation of middle-class, professional, educated Ashkenazim in its ranks. And some of its speakers were unable to keep from expressing their real (but racist) feeling that the "nice Israel" of the past (which never really existed) was being swept away.

Clearly it was in Peace Now's interest to avoid heightening Sephardi-Ashkenazi tensions, and to insist on the validity of their message for all Israelis. Unfortunately, nothing Peace Now might have done on its own would have defused these tensions, for the situation was too polarized. But the aftermath of the 1982 Lebanon War showed some signs of how fluid

---

17. Elsen, op.cit., interview with Yossi Shavit, November 8, 1978.

things could be. In July 1982, a public opinion poll showed 65.9% of the public justified all facets of the war, but by December this number was down to 34.4%.[18] With no tangible results to show for its involvement in the Lebanese quagmire, and Israeli soldiers getting killed or injured every other day, more Israelis questioned their government's handling of the entire affair.

There were also signs of shifts in the Sephardi community's loyalty to Begin. Some prominent Sephardi entertainers, like singer Shlomo Bar, came out strongly against the war and in favor of Peace Now's positions. Disaffection among local community leaders with the failure of the Likud's economic reforms also started to rise. Doves in the Tami (Moroccan) Party attacked Begin's war as "Ashkenazi imperialism" and tried to position themselves as the real bridge to peace with the Arabs. Still, Begin's grip on his Sephardi public largely remained firm. The process of healing the Sephardi-Ashkenazi split in Israeli society will probably take generations. Unfortunately, as rightwing politicians like Benjamin Netanyahu have since shown, the benefits of demagoguing the electorate with populist attacks on Ashkenazi "elites" and racist claims about Arabs tipping Israel's political balance outweighed the costs to Israel's social cohesion. In this respect, Peace Now's inability to extricate itself from its own origins in the elite and largely Ashkenazi ranks of the officer corps and the kibbutz movement significantly hindered its ability to shift a large portion of the Israeli public to its side.

What of Peace Now's ability to influence members of the Knesset, or even the possibility that it might have become a political party itself? Dedi Zucker criticized the movement for having been too wary of getting involved in the complicated and dirty world of Knesset politics, and he himself eventually chose to dive in, joining the Ratz Party (Movement for Civil Rights and Peace) in 1984 and serving in the Knesset from 1988-1999, eventually as part of the leftist Mapam Party.. "In politics you are sure that you are doing something," he said to me in the summer of 1982. "It's a fuller commitment. You want to change the situation? Join politics, devote your life, and start working."[19]

---

18. Shipler, op.cit., p.32.
19. *Ha'aretz*, March 7, 1983; Author interview with Dedi Zucker, August 18, 1982.

But could the movement have done more? Peace Now leaders from its early years acknowledged that, except for the occasional letter of support from members of Knesset, they did not attempt to formally deepen their ties with Knesset doves. There were two reasons for this. One was that they didn't want to weaken their broad appeal by appearing to be working on behalf of any given party. The other was that a decision to, say, mobilize support for Mapam in exchange for that party's support for Peace Now's political views, would have led to the internal fragmenting of Peace Now's activists along party lines (as well as the destruction of Peace Now's larger appeal). And in any case, the doves in the Knesset already existed and articulated positions consonant with Peace Now's views.

Fundamentally, the problem of influencing Knesset members was also rooted in the structure of Israel's electoral system. Party lists of candidates are drawn up by party leaders and elected by a nationwide vote, which means that members of the Knesset are primarily loyal to their party leadership and electoral power base (i.e., the kibbutzim, the religious community, various ethnic groups, business leaders). M.K.s do not have local constituencies to whom they are beholden on a day-to-day basis. Thus, the potential for lobbying-style efforts has always been quite low. At best, by mobilizing and strengthening support for the dovish position in the general public, Peace Now could strengthen the doves in the Knesset (causing them to fight for their views within their own parties), perhaps bring a few more out of the closet, and maybe convince them to break off from their parties to stand for the next elections as a new, peace party. But circumstances never really ripened to that point.

Thus Peace Now's leadership were basically correct in avoiding the Knesset role for their movement. As Janet Aviad said, "It would be burying Peace Now's strength to have it run."[20] Its strength as a movement, she argued, was that it could mobilize a united front around broad principles of agreement. As such, Abu Vilan said, it acted as an "umbrella for all the doves in Israel."[21] A bid for Knesset membership would have also meant the diversion of much time and energy into the creation of an organizational structure and the drafting of a platform on the broad range of issues

---

20. Author interview with Janet Aviad, August 3, 1982.
21. Author interview with Abu Vilan, August 5, 1982.

of concern to the Israeli public. And compared, for example, with the election of the Greens in Germany, the election of a Peace Now list would not have filled any vacuum on the Israeli left. The movement had a far more important role to play in the streets and in the schools, in the transformation of Israeli public opinion.

In addition, the existence of a broad "umbrella" movement like Peace Now generally anchored the Israeli peace movement. Other, smaller groups like Yesh Gvul, the Bir Zeit Solidarity Committee, the Sheli Party, and the group around *New Outlook* magazine were able to take more radical stands or use more radical tactics without fear of undermining public support for Peace Now. And the movement could use public reactions to the more radical actions of these smaller groups as a barometer to judge trends in public opinion. In this manner, a slow shift towards the left was created. For example, as Perry pointed out, because of Peace Now's early efforts, "It became possible to suggest a Palestinian state as an option."[22] Before Peace Now's existence, such a statement would have put one, in the public's mind, in the wilderness of the anti-Zionist left. The vindication of Peace Now's overarching strategy is that starting in the early 1980s, with the exception of the neo-fascist right-wing, such a stand became accepted as a viable Zionist position.

Peace Now's caution and moderation in its statements never stopped being a matter of much internal dispute for the movement. Some activists argued that it should take more radical positions and criticized it for behaving more like a "boy scout" movement with symbolic and legal protests than a serious opposition force.[23] However, its leaders always pointed out their dilemma. As Ita Gibson said to me, "If we sanction civil disobedience, refusal to do army service across the 'Green Line' [pre-1967 borders], we set a dangerous precedent. We don't want the army's discipline to break down."[24] The implication was that, someday, soldiers with right-wing views might refuse to carry out orders to dismantle settlements, for example.

In that respect, true to its origins, Peace Now viewed the integrity of the

---

22. Author interview with Moti Perry, January-February 1983.
23. *Ha'aretz*, March 7, 1983.
24. Author interview with Ita Gibson, July 20, 1982.

Israel Defense Forces as the country's most precious resource, and so resisted pressure to break its discipline. In addition, there was the justified fear that such an action would cause the delegitimization of Peace Now, and the loss of its hard-won public integrity. As Abu Vilan said to me, "When you are a dove in Israel, you have to argue from a defense point-of-view, and you have to show that you are not a PLO-lover, etc. Sometimes the only way to show it is that you are a fighter. This way we are morally stronger [with regards to the public]."[25]

The problem with this strategy is that it ceded much of the political initiative to Israel's rightwing. Until the debacle of the Lebanon invasion was evident, Begin was willing to take imperial initiatives without consulting the public or the Knesset, and he showed that was very capable of manipulating public opinion in his favor. The peace movement only slowly began to understand the implications of this. Said Tami Tzarfati in the summer of 1982, "Begin four years ago was not the same as Begin today. Now he's more powerful. This government doesn't take us into consideration, it governs by the masses. For the first time, we have to deal with the 'real right' ... At first I thought that if two thousand soldiers came back from the war opposing the defense minister, then he would have to go. Now I think they really don't care ... We're in for a very long rightwing consensus, government and spirit. We have to understand this."[26]

So, while opposing civil disobedience, everyone in the movement spoke of an imaginary and personal "red line" beyond which they would not go. It might be to refuse an order to shoot Palestinian civilians, or to refuse to tear gas Palestinian students, or to refuse to serve the occupied territories or Lebanon. But, for most, these "red lines" remained hypothetical. Peace Now's hesitation at drawing its "red line" over the 1982 war in Lebanon created much frustration in its ranks. Many of the members of the more radical Yesh Gvul group were Peace Now supporters who were dissatisfied with the movement's fence-sitting. Aside from the danger of Peace Now's fracturing over this question, there was the fact that, in despair, many young Peace Now supporters were beginning to consider leaving Israel. Said Shaul Markowitz: "When the war started, I felt]

---

25. Author interview with Abu Vilan, August 5, 1982.
26. Author interview with Tami Tzafarti, August 10, 1982.

despair, no hope ... I started to think ... what am I doing here? Many of the people in this country hate me—and they are ready to kill me ... And I know if there is a war I will have to go ... to defend what? ... Many people are thinking now about leaving. As a Zionist, it's hard to leave Israel. I was born here, I love this country."[27]

Peace Now built its strategy around not losing these young people. But at times it had little to offer besides hope and determination. Said Roni Siegel: "There are definitely signs of fascism rearing its ugly head. But you have to protect your rights or else they get taken away. If it comes to physical violence then that's what it comes to ... I believe you have to stand up for what you believe in.[28] And Janet Aviad added, "I don't see how I would stay in this country if things don't change ... I never intend to leave, however. I could not live here now and not be doing something."[29]

After its first turbulent five years of emergence, impact, dissipation and reemergence, Peace Now probably represented between 15% and 25% of the Israeli public, and perhaps had the passive support of another 10% or 15%. Because of its deliberate ambiguity, it undoubtedly reached beyond the supporters of the most left-wing parties in the Knesset to include many who voted for the Labor Party and other smaller centrist parties. This level of political support probably peaked in the early 1990s, when a coalition led by Yitzhak Rabin and his Labor Party came to power and when Israeli leaders took their greatest steps towards compromise with the Palestinian national movement, signing the Oslo Accords.

As it had in its early years, Peace Now played a significant role in preparing Israeli public opinion for a rapprochement with the Palestinians, coming out for recognition of the PLO in 1989, well before Rabin and Arafat's celebrated handshake on the White House lawn in 1993. But the lion's share of the credit for this shift has to be given to the PLO itself, which undertook its own process of internal debate and recalibration of its strategy after it was expelled from Lebanon in 1982 and then in the wake of the first Palestinian intifada in 1987-88–a topic well beyond the scope of this book.

---

27. Author interview with Shaul Markowitz, August 3, 1982.
28. Author interview with Roni Siegel, August 2, 1982.
29. Author interview with Janet Aviad, August 3, 1982.

Suffice it to say the Oslo process did not succeed. Rabin and Arafat never developed real trust in each other. Nor did they hammer out the kinds of pragmatic understandings that would have enabled them to take mutually reinforcing steps strengthening the path to the hard compromises necessary to fully end the binational conflict, as Ami Ayalon, a former head of Israel's Shin Bet internal security agency details eloquently in his memoir, *Friendly Fire*.[30] And then Rabin himself was soon gone, assassinated by a radical Jewish religious zealot in 1996.

Many other authors have illuminated how the hopes for a Israeli-Palestinian peace ran aground in the late 1990s, seemingly ending fully with Ariel Sharon's provocative visit to the Temple Mount in Jerusalem and the second intifada that then broke out in 2000. In particular, I would direct readers to Samy Cohen's 2019 book *Doves Among Hawks: Struggles of the Israeli Peace Movements*, which offers a careful and insightful parsing of the challenges and dilemmas that Peace Now faced in the Oslo years and the decades afterward. In his view, the movement was not just sidelined by the Oslo process but also hamstrung by its refusal to criticize a Labor Party leader, Yitzhak Rabin, even as he failed to stop settlements from expanding during the years when Israel and the PLO were supposed to working together towards a final comprehensive peace agreement. Rabin's successors, Shimon Peres and Ehud Barak, each lost further ground. And after the failure of the Camp David summit of 2000, Barak undercut the entire peace movement by declaring that Israel had "no partner for peace" on the other side.

And then, the waves of suicide bombings aimed at Israeli civilians broke the peace movement's credibility with most Israelis. As Cohen perceptively writes, "The feeling of fear inspired by the Palestinians and the lack of confidence in the 'other' that a great majority of Israelis refuse to consider a 'partner for peace' weigh far more heavily" on the reasons for the peace movement's decline than any variable like the shifting makeup of Israeli society in recent decades. "The facts speak for themselves: all those who have attempted to put forward solutions to the Israeli–Palestinian conflict have been marginalized within Israeli society; they have

---

30. Ami Ayalon, *Friendly Fire: How Israel Became its Worst Enemy* (Scribe Publications Ltd, 2020)

been put out to pasture for reasons to do with the country's collective psychology. Even Yitzhak Rabin was unable to disarm that fear."[31]

But as Tamar S. Hermann argues in her 2009 book *The Israeli Peace Movement: A Shattered Dream*, "Despite being long located on the political periphery, the movement has been a significant factor in influencing the climate of opinion in Israel by persistently putting forward some unconventional and much contested alternative readings of the conflict, thereby cultivating the ground for the transformation from armed conflict to peace negotiations." Later, when Oslo collapsed, Hermann writes that the peace movement "was apparently the only political body in Israel, perhaps in the region, that continued to keep the ashes of the hope for peace in the future warm."[32]

This determination was always at the heart of Peace Now. The movement that I encountered most closely in its early years, as described in the preceding pages, had no illusions about the struggle ahead—its leaders spoke in terms of years of commitment. In that respect, they were the carriers of the same dream and hope that has inspired peace-loving people the world over. "I care very much to be able to face a Palestinian and to say I was okay," Janet Aviad said to me in the summer of 1982. It is this fundamental moral insight—that to heal themselves and their society Israelis must face head on The Other that they have ignored, oppressed and sought to exterminate, and learn to live with him or her as a fellow human being—that keeps Peace Now on the right track. As Mordecai Bar-On wrote, "If you have an enemy, you must find a way to make peace, not to keep that enemy an enemy."[33] And Janet Aviad, "Now we have to see where to go ... it's not over ... it's far from over."[34]

---

31. Samy Cohen, *Doves Among Hawks: Struggles of the Israeli Peace Movements*, p. 6.
32. Tamas S. Hermann, *The Israeli Peace Movement: A Shattered Dream* (Cambridge: Cambridge University Press, 2009), p. 7.
33. Baron, op. cit.
34. Author interview with Janet Aviad, August 3, 1982.

CHAPTER 8
EPILOGUE

AFTER OCTOBER 7, CAN WE HAVE PEACE NOW, OR EVER?

TODAY, Peace Now's staff works out of an office in the basement of a residential building in north Tel Aviv, which I visited with a delegation from its sister organization, Americans for Peace Now[1], in the spring of 2024. Even though the neighborhood is pretty left-leaning, there's no sign outside that this is the headquarters of one of Israel's oldest peace organizations. Inside is a low-ceilinged warren of small offices that serve as home for about a half-dozen core staff, many of whom are there to greet our delegation. The basement floor tiles are heavily scuffed and the upholstery on all the chairs in the crowded conference room is worn down and torn.

Still, the spirit of the movement is evident. All the walls are festooned with photos of past rallies—a huge 2007 demonstration against the occupation marking its 50th anniversary, a photo of a baby at a demo holding a sign reading (in Hebrew) "The Right won't silence me"; a shot of US actor Mandy Patinkin, a longtime supporter, addressing a Peace Now meeting; and many pictures of volunteers. One storage room is stuffed with banners, drums and megaphones—the paraphernalia of veteran street protestors—along with piles of Peace Now t-shirts and stickers marking the 25th anniversary of Rabin's assassination. On the restroom door,

---

1. Americans for Peace Now merged with another progressive Zionist group, Ameinu, in late 2024, taking a new name: New Jewish Narrative.

someone with a wry sense of humor has put up a sign reading: "L'hashtin Ackshav—Piss Now."

Lior Amihai, Peace Now's current executive director, gives me a few minutes of his time before our group meeting formally begins. He's a youthful-looking 39-year-old, with brown hair, a thin beard and a solidarity bracelet on his wrist for the hostages being held by Hamas in Gaza in the wake of the October 7th attack. I ask him what it is like to be running such a storied organization. Until 2000, he tells me, Peace Now was a huge factor in Israeli society. It was constantly holding meetings with Palestinians, negotiating with them, and doing whatever it could to try to advance the prospect of co-existence opened by the Oslo Accords of the early 1990s. But then, after the collapse of peace talks at the end of 2000 and the breakout of the second intifada, "We lost the politics," Amihai admitted. Israeli Prime Minister Ehud Barak's churlish declaration that there was "no one to talk to" as a partner for peace—along with the toll from dozens of suicide bombings organized by Hamas—caused most of the peace camp to disappear. The Labor party chose to join the next government as a junior partner to Ariel Sharon (whose brazen decision to visit the Temple Mount triggered the second intifada) and parties further to the left lost most of their seats in the Knesset.

Now, Amihai noted, "There's no Meretz"–the old coalition party that had absorbed the remnants of the socialist-Zionist left—and "only one Labor M.K. who dares to speak out, Gilad Kariv." He added that there was one other M.K. who had worked in the past for Peace Now, but she didn't make fighting the occupation her main agenda. Still, he argued that "Peace Now is still relevant." The war with Hamas in Gaza had exposed "an elephant in the room that people thought they could ignore," he said, meaning the unresolved Palestinian problem. And through all the years, even with the challenges of sustaining support for a two-state solution in the wake of the second intifada, "Peace Now didn't dissolve," he said. "We kept up the public fight."

He also noted that the international community hadn't forgotten either. Indeed, when I asked him how Peace Now managed to pay its staff— something it didn't have in its early years—he said that alongside some Israeli donors, much of its support came from countries that funded its primary project, Settlement Watch, along with support from sister organizations like Americans for Peace Now.

I asked Amihai to describe how the Peace Now of 2024 understood its theory of change, how it would win over public opinion. "The cause is strong enough," he declared, arguing that there was no other plausible resolution to the conflict. "We try to sense the public mood and to see how, in the most effective way, we can respond to it," he added, an echo of something Peace Now veteran Janet Aviad had said to me years ago about the organization's role as a channel as well as a catalyst.

In the year prior to the October 7 attack, while Israel was consumed with weekly anti-government demonstrations focused on opposing Prime Minister Bibi Netanyahu's effort to ram through anti-democratic legislation that would neuter the country's independent judiciary, Peace Now faced a challenge. That was because the occupation was not the primary focus of the pro-democracy movement. But Amihai saw that period as a time of great promise. "We went to the demonstrations and saw them as an opportunity to inject our issues," he told me. But he admitted that the democracy movement did not put enough emphasis on the two-state solution.

Later that afternoon our delegation met with a mix of Peace Now's current leaders and veteran activists. Here Amihai was more explicit about the challenge the movement faces. "It's almost contradictory to be at Peace Now today," he said. Until October 7, no one wanted to address the Palestinian issue or advancing a two-state solution, especially in the wake of the so-called Abraham Accords brokered by the Trump administration, that led to normalized relations between Israel and several Arab countries. Now, he said, "the two-state solution is back on the international agenda, and the conflict, at least, is back on the Israeli agenda." He added, "It's our moment to shine. Our main mission has to be how to mobilize and convince the public that the two-state solution is the only way to resolve the conflict."

Yariv Oppenheimer, a former executive director of Peace Now, agreed, with characteristic Israeli humor. "There are times when this organization is needed, and there are times when it is really, really needed," he said wryly. "Now we are really needed to work on Israeli public opinion. It's a huge challenge. The right-wing and Israeli media are trying to silence this approach. It's a life-or-death issue for us and the country."

Gary Brenner, a longtime Peace Now activist who I had met and interviewed back in 1982, chimed in as well. "We need to talk about the day after [the Gaza war ends]," he noted. "Anyone who raises it ultimately will get to the two-state solution." As for Netanyahu, who insists at every opportunity that he will never allow a Palestinian state to be created alongside Israel, Brenner declared, "Bibi says he is speaking for the public, but it's a blatant lie. There's an opportunity here."

———

OCTOBER 7 AND THE INTENSIFICATION OF THE ISRAEL-PALESTINE BINARY

It is true that the October 7 terrorist attack by Hamas and Israel's subsequent war on Gaza has revived global interest in the Israel-Palestine conflict and intensified engagement across the spectrum of concerned and affected parties. But my visit to Israel-Palestine with Americans for Peace Now didn't make me more optimistic about the prospects for reaching a compromise and achieving some kind of peaceful co-existence, whether it's called a "two-state solution" or some other form of power- and land-sharing.

Two forces are contending for the future of this troubled land. The first are those Israeli Jews and Palestinian Arabs who want to control *all the land* from "the river to the sea" for their people only. While ethnonationalism is at the heart of each of these groups, messianic and fundamentalist religion is increasingly powering their actions—whether that is of the Jewish settlers terrorizing Palestinians across the West Bank or Hamas militia shooting rockets at Israelis, storming their kibbutzim and taking hostages. For obvious reasons, we couldn't safely visit Gaza or the major Palestinian cities in the West Bank during our 2024 trip, but our encounters in Area C–the part of the West Bank fully controlled by the Israeli military–made clear how much the settlement movement has been empowered and emboldened in recent years.

On the first day of our tour, a U.S. official based in Jerusalem joined us for lunch. Speaking on background, he painted a stark picture. There had been a surge in settler violence against Palestinians in the West Bank since October 7, he said. New "rapid response" units there set up by the IDF are essentially settler militias. They are very few investigations of their actions, so they operate within a "culture of impunity." And while the Biden Administration's imposition of travel restrictions and sanctions on a handful of violent settlers was a promising intervention, "more tranches of designees could be announced and organizations could be named too," this official said, referring to groups like the "hilltop youth" and La Familia, a violent soccer gang aligned with the far-right. Not enough was being done to control them, he was telling us.

"Settler violence and terrorism are two sides of the same coin," the official said. "Could Israel turn this off if it wanted? Of course it could." He pointed to how the government uses administrative detention to hold without trial Palestinians it deems dangerous. "There's no reason they can't do that with settlers too." The official said they'd like to see the new Biden sanctions extended to include financial flows to the settler movement, since "material support" for violent settlers is indeed covered by the White House's executive order.

As for the situation in Gaza, the U.S. official didn't mince words. He told us that since October 7 he and his colleagues had worked on three main priorities. First, getting US citizens there out. About 450 out of about 600 have been aided. Second, making sure that the Israelis don't over-react to the attack. "I'm not sure how successful we've been," he said drily. And third, getting humanitarian aid in. He talked about how Secretary of State Antony Blinken had worked late into the night on one of his many visits to the region pushing the Israelis to up the number of trucks from three a day to twenty or thirty, but admitted it was still a disaster. And the post-war situation, the official said, was likely to be grim. "This is going to cost billions and billions to rebuild," they said. "The most likely scenario [for Gaza] is Mogadishu on the Mediterranean."

"The only people with a long-term strategic plan here is the settler movement," this American official concluded. That was the perfect transition to our next meeting, with lawyer Daniel Seidemann, an expert on Jerusalem's history and development who works closely with Peace Now. With him we got a fast in-depth seminar on how the intermeshed religious communities of Jerusalem were being pushed toward a conflagration by what he called "religious pyromaniacs." We started at his office, where he showed us a new three-dimensional model of the city mapping 450 of its holy sites that shows how Jews, Muslims and Christians all intermingle. "No one [religion] can say that 'we exclusively own Jerusalem'." The map leaves out settlements and Jewish religious sites built after 1948, he noted.

For a while after the 1967 war, when Israel conquered the Old City and East Jerusalem, it avoided changing the status quo. Israeli flags flew only briefly over the mosques captured in the Six Day War, since Moshe Dayan, Israel's defense minister, ordered that they be immediately taken down. "We don't need a holy war," Dayan declared. Still, Israel annexed East Jerusalem and built ten new neighborhoods, adding 230,000 Jews to its Palestinian population. But this was not done by displacing Palestinians from their homes.

That is now changing. "What was unthinkable has now become thinkable," Seidemann said, pointing to settler efforts to encircle Palestinian East Jerusalem with building takeovers, new "national parks" and sites dedicated to celebrating nationalistic symbols. The problem today, he told us, "is the ascendancy of those who weaponize faith. Often it is incendiary." The first organization to pay attention to his work, which started in the early 1990s when religious settlers started to lay claim to the East Jerusalem neighborhood of Silwan, was the Pentagon. "They were the first to understand, because they were used to seeing pictures of the al-Aqsa mosque of Jerusalem on the walls of sheikhs in Afghanistan," he said.

The good news, he says, is "The border still exists." On the holy day of Yom Kippur, when all of Jewish Israel shuts down, checkpoints go up across Jerusalem that restrict Palestinians to driving only in their part of the city. This, he said, shows that most of the time the two national groups drive on different streets, send their kids to different schools, and so on— and the Israeli authorities are well aware of where to draw the lines. And if the old 1967 border, the so-called Green Line on maps, still exists in social practice, then it can be redrawn as a political boundary. Driving around the eastern quadrant of the city, Seidemann showed us how geography might still be destiny. Thanks in part to the vigilance of groups like Peace Now and activists like Seidemann, governments like the United States had still managed to block Israel from effectively cutting the West Bank in half, preventing a future Palestinian state from being one contiguous body.

We have not yet crossed the point of no return, when a two-state solution becomes impossible, Seidemann was telling us. But the ingredients for

an explosion and a rapid devolution of the status quo were all in place. As
the US diplomat also noted, the international community had almost no
one inside the Israeli government to talk with, let alone listen to, beyond
elements of the army and the Shin Bet, who both understand that the occupation is the biggest threat to Israel's security. The religious pyromaniacs
who are in leadership positions in the Israeli government, like national
security minister Itamar Ben-Gvir, and their counterparts in Hamas and in
Iran, were hoping for a bigger confrontation. God will be of no help if that
happens.

This situation has gotten markedly worse since Trump returned to the
White House. His ambassador to Israel, Mike Huckabee, is a full-blown
Christian Zionist who emphatically denies Palestinian peoplehood.
"There's no such thing as a settlement," he likes to say. "They're communities. They're neighborhoods. They're cities. There's no such thing as an
occupation."[2] Biden's sanctions on violent settlers have been revoked by
Trump, and in August of 2025 the Netanyahu government approved plans
to build the extension of the Ma'ale Adumim settlement that architect
Daniel Seidmann had explained to us would be the death-blow to a
contiguous West Bank Palestinian state. In response, Peace Now
denounced the decision, saying it would lead to a "binational apartheid
state."[3]

I saw more than my share of destruction in just a few days on that
Americans for Peace Now tour in 2024. Three times in five days I stood in
front of wrecked houses, thinking about the ruined lives they represent.
First, in the Negev desert at Kibbutz Be'eri in the south along the border
with Gaza, where Hamas terrorists and other Gazans ran amok, brutally
killing hundreds of Israeli civilians—including dedicated peace activists
like Vivian Silver, one of the founders of Women Wage Peace, a Jewish-
Arab group. Second, a day later, in the verdant mountains of the West
Bank, where a village of several dozen Bedouin lay abandoned after Jewish

2. Jesus Mesa, "Settlers Rejoice as Hard-Liner Mike Huckabee Picked for Israel Ambassador,"
Newsweek, November 12, 2024, https://www.newsweek.com/israeli-settlers-react-mike-huck
abee-ambassador-israel-1984770.
3. Jeremy Sharon, "E1 settlement project widely condemned, but is it fatal to the two-state
solution idea?" *The Times of Israel*, August 25, 2025, https://www.timesofisrael.com/e1-settle
ment-project-widely-condemned-but-is-it-fatal-to-two-state-solution-idea/.

147

settlers built outposts encroaching on their grazing land, choked off their livelihood and then violently intimidated them into leaving. And third, in Israeli-annexed East Jerusalem, where residents of the Palestinian village of al-Walaja cleaned out the ruins of one house that the authorities demolished a week earlier and another stood in front of her similarly flattened home and told us how her life was destroyed a year ago.

No, I am not suggesting that these three stories are equivalent. Hamas's wanton murder spree on October 7 is not the precise moral equivalent of the Jewish settlement movement's steady encroachment on Palestinian life and property, or the Israeli government's bureaucratic imposition of sudden home demolitions on villagers whose only crime is building on their own land without a formal permit—which they can't get because, following Kafka's advice, the Israelis authorities refuse to produce a development plan for the village. What Hamas did in one day was crueler and more destructive. But the result is the same: more destroyed lives. And with each turn in this cycle of violent action and reaction, the rejectionists on both sides get stronger. Israel's massive response in Gaza, an overkill that was fueled by a need for revenge but with every subsequent week looked more and more like deliberate ethnic cleansing, if not outright genocide, has made the situation markedly worse.

It's a slender thread to hang on, but there is another force also contending for the future in Israel-Palestine, people working for equality and security for both peoples, whether that is in a two-state solution or in the development of a shared society. Unlike the peace dialogue groups of the late 1990s, which melted away after the suicide bombings of the second intifada, the new generation of "shared society" groups that have arisen since then held their own during the inter-communal riots of May 2021, when rightwing Jewish youth and radical Palestinian youth attacked the other side in the streets of several mixed Jewish-Arab cities inside Israel proper. After October 7, many of these groups formed rapid response networks to quickly respond to hyper-local flare-ups and tamp down rumors before they could generate violence or go viral on social media.

On one afternoon of our trip, we met Mohammed Faheli, the director of the Clore Jewish-Arab Community Center in Akko, which provides low-cost services and classes to 500 Arab and Jewish families in that mixed city. Akko, which has grown metastatically like the rest of Israel since I spent six months on nearby Kibbutz Shomrat back in 1980, has been riven more than once by violence between the communities. Faheli told us how, as a young teen, he had made friends while working at a nearby kibbutz, whose members then started giving him wagon loads of fresh produce to help his family. Then, a few years later, while working at a Texas hotel, its Jewish owner heard him speaking Hebrew and asked him to tutor his children. That led to an even bigger friendship, and when he returned to Akko the hotel owner gave him $5,000 to buy his first home in Akko.

Those acts of generosity changed his life and led him to open the community center. It's a place, Faheli proudly noted, where Jewish and Arab families sit together, eat together, and play together. "We don't have a security guard here," he noted. "Everywhere you go in Israel, Jewish places have security guards. We don't because we aren't afraid of each other," he declared. "The only solution is to live with each other."

On one of my last days in Israel-Palestine, I sat in a café at the Beilenson Hospital complex in Petah Tikva, waiting for an old friend of mine to finish a doctor's appointment. The hospitals in Israel-Palestine are among the most integrated places in the whole country, with roughly half the doctors and nurses coming from the Palestinian Arab community. I spied an Israeli nurse talking in Hebrew talking to an Arab colleague who was wearing a traditional scarf covering her hair. I tried to quickly snap a picture as they walked by, but even this moment of comity was too fleeting for me to capture.

The hundred-year war between Jews and Arabs for control of this tormented land doesn't have to continue forever. But somehow, the national religious fanatics of both sides must be drained of their energy first. That starts with rejecting the emotional temptations of revenge and tribalism. As Vice President Kamala Harris said after she met with Israeli Prime Minister Netanyahu during his July 2024 visit to the US, "The war in Gaza is not a binary issue, however, too often the conversation is binary, when the reality is anything but."[4]

---

4. "Remarks by Vice President Harris Following Meeting with Prime Minister Benjamin Netanyahu of Israel", July 25, 2024, https://bidenwhitehouse.archives.gov/briefing-room/speeches-remarks/2024/07/25/remarks-by-vice-president-harris-following-meeting-with-prime-minister-benjamin-netanyahu-of-israel/.

A NEW GENERATION OF ISRAELI-PALESTINIAN ORGANIZING RISES

What gives me some hope about the prospect for peace is not just the longevity and tenacity of organizations like Peace Now, but also the rise of a new generation of joint Israeli-Palestinian political organizing. No group better evinces this than Standing Together, a Jewish-Arab social movement. "We need a new political current in Israel, a new story," Sally Abed, a Palestinian Arab citizen of Israel who is one of its founders, told an audience of mostly progressive Jewish activists in New York, a few weeks after October 7. "Our mission is to build a new majority around peace, equality for all, and ending the occupation." This, she says, can only come about by convincing Israelis, Jews and Arabs alike, that it is in their interest to do so. How? By building a distributed movement with thousands of members organized in local chapters across the country and in the universities, one of the few places other than Israel's so-called "mixed" cities where young Israeli Jews and Palestinians meet as peers.

Here's how Standing Together weaves anti-occupation and pro-equality work into a message that can reach beyond the choir. Much of it reminds me of how early Peace Now organizers tried to build common ground with Israel's Sephardi underclass:

> "The current socio-political reality in Israel is unbearable. Unending occupation feeds violence, fear, and hatred between Israelis and Palestinians. Economic inequality is widening. Poverty is deepening. Israel's Palestinian minority faces increasing discrimination. Women, Mizrahim [Israelis who trace their roots to Arab countries], immigrants, the LGBTQ+ community, the elderly, and people with disabilities are marginalized socially, economically, and politically. Working people must labor for ever longer hours at stagnating wages while the cost of living continues to soar even higher. Rather than seriously address these problems, our political leaders use fear and racism to divide us. Instead of providing genuine security solutions, they deliver never-ending wars. Rather than serve the majority, they look out only for the rich. Our government is increasingly disconnected and corrupt. Israeli society is in a deep crisis."[5]

---

5. "About Us," Standing Together, https://www.standing-together.org/en/about-en.

Alon-Lee Green, another co-founder of Standing Together, is also not a newcomer to political organizing in Israel. In 2011, he was one of the leaders of the country's "social protest" movement, an echo of the Occupy and Indignado flowerings that grew to huge proportions there, mobilizing half a million Israelis at its peak. But that movement was effectively neutered after Prime Minister Netanyahu appointed a commission of economists to study the problem of growing inequality and people folded up their tents and went home. In 2015, after Netanyahu declared that he planned to forever control "all of the territory" and that "we will forever live by the sword,"[6] Green decided to try to build a vessel that acknowledge the pain of *both* Israelis and Palestinians, that could grow and absorb people from both communities simultaneously and set them together on a different path.

"We are fortunate to be in this catastrophic moment with an organized movement," he said at that same meeting, "one that can keep people in the middle." Green and Abed didn't mince words about what the war was doing to Israeli Jews and Arabs. "On October 7, Hamas committed a massacre," Green said. "They had no mercy. Our society is in a very deep state of trauma. People feel unsafe in their own homes." And since then, on top of the thousands killed by Israel's invasion of Gaza, he added, "Some political forces are losing no time to advance the craziest, messianic ideas imaginable." While Israel wages war with Hamas, another war is being fought over what kind of society Israel will be, between a "Jewish supremacist government" that wants to undermine the country's independent judiciary, narrow its democracy, and give Jewish settlers free rein to terrorize Palestinians in the West Bank, and the kind of tolerant, open and equal civil society Standing Together is fighting for.

Itamir Ben-Gvir, the far-right minister who oversees the country's police forces, has handed out tens of thousands of guns to local "civil defense" groups inside Israel, backed by groups who want to stoke tensions between Jews and Arabs, Green told us. These same groups are also targeting leaders of Israel's pro-democracy movement, calling them "traitors who should be hung from the highest tree," for how they suppos-

---

6. Barak Ravid, "Netanyahu: I Don't Want a Binational State, but We Need to Control All of the Territory for the Foreseeable Future," *Ha'aretz*, October 26, 2015.

edly weakened the country before the Hamas attack, Green added. To respond, Standing Together had been building Arab-Jewish solidarity groups and was posting its distinctive, purple-colored posters reading "together" in Hebrew and Arabic everywhere it can. In the weeks after October 7, it organized four solidarity rallies in mixed cities across the country, giving people a place to mourn together and offer each other mutual support. "What we can do is try to de-escalate the violence and hostilities between the two communities," Abed noted, "which also humanizes the other in the process."

This is exceedingly important work, and it was being made more difficult by a growing crackdown on Palestinian free speech inside Israel and a hardening of Jewish Israeli public opinion as the war expanded. "If you follow 'News from Palestine' on your Instagram account, someone can take a picture of that and report you," Green said, "and then you can lose your job, or get expelled from university." This is happening by the thousands, he added. Abed chimed in: "Palestinians in Israel are trying to erase themselves right now," fearful of having an opinion or expressing solidarity "with our people." This concerns her greatly, because Israeli Palestinians have a crucial role to play in building a new peace camp.

But as world opinion turned harshly against Israel, Jewish Israelis who feel they have to defend themselves from Hamas's terrorism were being radicalized in the other direction. "On the evening news, it's becoming normalized to say that we should wipe out all of Gaza," Green worried. "The question is whether we can remain human and moral in this moment." I don't think it's a coincidence that Green and Abed didn't lead with words like "genocide," "ethnic cleansing" or "apartheid"—I'm not even sure they used them once during that whole meeting in New York. They are serious people trying to actually get something done.

"We are in a world with just two options," Green declared at one point. Either an "endless war, an endless cycle of blood," or an Israel-Palestinian peace agreement. And to give that second option a chance, he and Abed both brought a critical message to progressives in America: The zero-sum game of competing oppressions, of competing unilateral claims to justice, is doomed. Green was vociferous on this point. "The whole of Israeli society is being completely overlooked" in the global debate over the war, he said. "And no one is going anywhere. The only question that needs to be asked is how we can live together."

People like him in Israel are very aware of how the left in America and other parts of the world is talking about them, and they insisted it wasn't helping. "You can call me a colonizer or a settler," he declared, "but I'm not going anywhere. And neither are the Palestinians." When people chant, "Palestine will be free," he said, "we Israelis hear, 'without you.' In the same way that a lot of Palestinians hear the ministers in Bibi's government speak and think they want to do the same thing to them." The problem as they both see it is that we are caught between two polar opposites. "Hamas believes in Greater Palestine," Green said. "And on the other side we have people who believe in the idea of Greater Israel." Indeed, that concept is in the charter of Netanyahu's Likud Party. "Both sides have very problematic governing bodies," he added.

Abed denounced the academic left's pronouncements on the conflict. "It's so theorized—colonized and colonizers—without any connection to how you build a change on the ground." Green cut in, "We are not here to entertain you," alluding to how performative the pro-Palestinian protest movement appears to him. "We are going to stay here." I asked them how they, as people on the left, had managed to avoid the simplistic binary that sees the Israelis as the oppressors with more power and the Palestinians as the oppressed with less power, which leads to acting like the oppressor can do nothing right and the oppressed can do no wrong.

"We live together," Abed said. "I know the conversation here. And I have decided to take responsibility for my society, instead of just saying 'Free Palestine.'" She paused, and then offered an example of what her lived reality of Jewish-Arab solidarity actually felt like. "One of our leaders in Standing Together, Chaim Katzman, he was at Masafer Yatta [a collection of Palestinian villages in the southern West Bank that the Israeli government is demolishing] every week." Her voice caught. "And they [Hamas] shot him dead." Everyone in the room heaved a little. Abed apologized for "triggering" anyone's trauma and a woman seated near her responded that she needn't apologize, that we are all "triggered as fuck."

Then Abed gathered herself. "Other than proving you are more right, what is your mission?" Abed asked of the Palestine solidarity movement. "If it's not helping, then shut the fuck up." She went on, "The damage it is doing to our work; it's fueling so much hate." In her view, the shriller the language deployed against Israeli policies or the country itself, the more hardliners in the government and in public opinion were strengthened. "The global left has to be synced with what we need. Holding a sign with the Israeli flag in a garbage can—how does that help at all? Other than making you feel righteous. It's heartbreaking to me how distant I feel from Palestinian-Americans here."

It's high time we listened more to people closest to the conflict, especially those dedicated to co-existence, instead of the conflict entrepreneurs whipping up anger and polarization. Unfortunately, the Israel-Palestine conflict in America has become a version of what my friend, the political scientist Lee Drutman, writing in a different context, has called the "two-party doom loop."[7] He coined that phrase to describe the current American political dynamic, where Republicans and Democrats have organized themselves into two warring camps driven by their most passionate adherents, and where each side's extremes generates fuel for the other side, intensifying the conflict. No one listens in good faith to the other side, no one searches for consensus, and people at the poles reap rewards while people in the middle get punished.

In the Israel-Palestine version of the doom loop, the pro-Israel lobby group AIPAC announcing it will spend $100 million to take out members of Congress it deems too radical helps those very members targeted also raise money in response, and the pro-Palestine statements made by those same members helps AIPAC raise more money. An anti-Zionist activist who posts a spreadsheet list of Zionist authors to boycott and anti-Zionist authors to support generates more evidence for the pro-Israel side of "rising antisemitism" as much as it adds energy to the boycott crowd. Rinse and repeat, rinse and repeat. Instead of building an antiwar movement in the United States to complement the efforts of groups like Standing Together, well-intentioned activists have chosen instead to polarize the issue further. That may be good for their individual organizations' membership recruitment and fundraising efforts, but as a theory of change

---

7. Lee Drutman, *Breaking the Two-Party Doom Loop: The Case for Multiparty Democracy in America*, Oxford University Press, 2020.

it is only delivering an intensification of the conflict and a hardening of positions on all sides.

As I finish these pages, Israeli Prime Minister Benjamin Netanyahu has chosen to break another cease-fire between Israel and Hamas in Gaza, and the IDF is embarking on a mission to "conquer and control" the territory, with plans to demolish whatever buildings are still standing and force Gaza's two million civilians into so-called "humanitarian cities" under tight military control, with the expectation that this will finally force Hamas to surrender. Perhaps this will happen; more likely such harsh steps will just generate more resistance, which is what Hamas–the "Islamic Resistance Movement"—literally means.

Inside Israel, since early 2025 thousands of military reservists have been circulating and publishing open letters declaring their refusal to continue down this path, a striking echo of the Officers' Letter that began Peace Now's rise decades ago.[8] In July, more than seventy percent of the Israeli public said they favored an end to the war and the trading of all the hostages still held by Hamas for thousands of Palestinian prisoners held by Israel.[9] But Netanyahu's political coalition showed no sign of breaking, and with Trump talking openly of moving a million or more Palestinians out of Gaza, it seems unlikely that there will be any change in Israel's current expansionist and eliminationist path until new Knesset elections occur in the fall of 2026.

As they have so many times in this long binational conflict, extremists on both sides keep reinforcing each other. The joint poll by the Palestinian Center for Policy and Survey Research (PSR) in Ramallah and the International Program in Conflict Resolution and Mediation at Tel Aviv University from September 2024 that I cited in this book's introduction makes for extremely depressing reading if you only focus on its main finding–that supermajorities of Israelis and Palestinians currently believe the

---

8. PBS, "Protest letters from former Israeli soldiers reveal major rifts over ongoing war in Gaza," April 18, 2025, https://www.pbs.org/newshour/world/protest-letters-from-former-israeli-soldiers-reveal-major-rifts-over-ongoing-war-in-gaza.

9. "Breaking with PM, 74% of Israelis back war-ending deal to free all hostages — poll," *Times of Israel*, July 11, 2025, https://www.timesofisrael.com/breaking-with-pm-74-of-israelis-back-war-ending-deal-to-free-all-hostages-poll/.

other side is committed to their complete destruction, and therefore they must accordingly steel themselves for more war and more resistance.

Successful peace movements are rare, but they succeed when they find ways to break the cycle of violence and polarization and replace it with one that reinforces the efforts of moderates to achieve a compromise. And that will mean accepting imperfection and incomplete resolutions. But as Benjamin Franklin said centuries ago, "There never was a good war or a bad peace."[10] Maybe, if this latest round in the Israeli-Palestinian Hundred Years War ever dies down, everyone will be able to fully see the wreckage that has been wrought by the fanatics. Only then may both sides be ready to learn that lesson.

---

10. Letter from Benjamin Franklin to Josiah Quincy, Sr., 11 September 1783, https://founders.archives.gov/documents/Franklin/01-40-02-0385.

BIBLIOGRAPHY

NEWSPAPERS AND PERIODICALS

Al Ha'mishmar
Davar
Ha'aretz
Hotam
Israleft News Service
The Jerusalem Post
The Jerusalem Post International Edition
Ma'ariv
Middle East International
The Middle East Reporter
Monitin
The New York Times
The Village Voice
The World Today
Yediot Aharonot

———

INTERVIEWS

Gary Brenner, Kibbutz Artzi-Peace Now (Tel Aviv), July 12, 1982.
Yossi Ben-Artzi, Peace Now (Haifa), July 13, 1982.
Andre Draznin, Yesh Gvul, January 1984.
lta Gibson, Peace Now (Jerusalem), July 20, 1982.
Roni Siegel, Peace Now (Jerusalem), August 2, 1982.
Rafi Greenberg, Peace Now (Jerusalem), August 2, 1982.
Janet Aviad, Peace Now (Jerusalem), August 3, 1982.
Shaul Markowitz, Peace Now (Jerusalem), August 3, 1982.
Avraham Schenker, Jewish Agency (Tel Aviv), August 4, 1982.
Chaika Grossman, M.K. Mapam (Tel Aviv), August 4, 1982.
Abu Vilan, Peace Now (Kibbutz Negba), August 5, 1982.
Tsali Reshef, Peace Now, January 1984.
Hillel Schenker, New Outlook, (Tel Aviv), August 6, 1982.
Arieh Palgi, author of *Shalom V'Lo Yotair* (Peace and No More), (Tel Aviv), August 10, 1982 .
Gadi Elgazi, member of the "Group of 27" resisters to service in the occupied territories (Kibbutz Adamit), August 12, 1982.
Dedi Zucker, Peace Now, Citizens Rights Movement (Jerusalem), August 18, 1982
Moti Perry, Peace Now (Princeton), January-February 1983.

TITLES

Abu-Lughod, Ibrahim, ed., *The Transformation of Palestine*, Evanston: Northwestern University Press, 1971.

Avineri, Shlomo, *The Making of Modern Zionism*, N.Y.: Basic Books, Inc., 1981.

Ayalon, Ami, *Friendly Fire: How Israel Became its Worst Enemy*, Lebanon, New Hampshire: Scribe Publications Ltd, 2020.

Bar-On, Mordecai, *In Pursuit of Peace*, Washington, DC: US Institute of Peace, 1996.

Begin, Menachem, *The Revolt*, Tel Aviv: Hadar Publishing, 1964.

Beinart, Peter, *Being Jewish After the Destruction of Gaza*, N.Y.: Alfred Knopf, 2025.

Cohen, Samy, *Doves Among Hawks: Struggles of the Israeli Peace Movements*, London: Hurst Publishers, 2019.

Curtis, Michael and Mordecai Chertoff, eds., *Israel: Social Structure and Change*, New Brunswick: Transaction Books, 1973.

Drutman, Lee, *Breaking the Two-Party Doom Loop: The Case for Multiparty Democracy*, N.Y.: Oxford University Press, 2020.

Eisenstadt, S.N., *Israeli Society*, N.Y.: Basic Books, Inc., 1967.

Elon, Amos, *The Israelis: Founders and Sons*, London: Sphere Books Limited, 1971.

Elsen, Susan, *Shalom Achshav—The Peace Now Movement in Israel: A Bus on the Road to Peace*, unpublished senior thesis, History Department, Princeton University, April 18, 1979;

Flink, Salomon J., *Israel: Chaos and Challenge*, Ramat Gan: Turtledove Publishing, 1979.

Frankel, William, *Israel Observed: An Anatomy of the State*, USA: Thames and Hudson, 1980.

Giner, Fanny, *Socio-Economic Disparities in Israel*, Tel Aviv: University Publishing Projects, Ltd., 1979.

Golany, B., *Statehood and Zionism*, N.Y.: New Zionist Organization of America, 1958.

Haber, Eitan, Ze'ev Schiff and Ehud Yaari, *The Year of the Dove*, USA: Bantam Books, 1979.

Halabi, Rafik, *The West Bank Story*, N. Y.: Harcourt Brace Jovanovich, Pub!., 1981.

Halpern, Ben, *The Idea of the Jewish State*, Cambridge: Harvard University Press, 1961.

Harkabi, Yehoshafat, *The Bar Kokhba Syndrome: Risk and Realism In International Politics*, Chappaqua, N. Y.: Rossel Books, 1983.

Heller, Mark A., *A Palestinian State: The Implications for Israel*, Cambridge: Harvard University Press, 1983.

Hermann, Tamar, *The Israeli Peace Movement: A Shattered Dream*, Cambridge: Cambridge University Press, 2009.

Hertzberg, Arthur, ed., *The Zionist Idea*, N.Y.: Atheneum, 1959.

Horowitz, Dan and Moshe Lissak, *Origins of the Israeli Polity*, Chicago: University of Chicago Press, 1978.

Hurewitz, J.C., *The Struggle for Palestine*, N.Y.: Schocken Books, 1950.

International Institute for Strategic Studies, *The Military Balance—1981*.

Isaac, Rael Jean, *Israel Divided: Ideological Politics in the Jewish State*, Baltimore: The Johns Hopkins University Press, 1976.

Kahane, Meir, *They Must Go*, N. Y.: Grosset and Dunlap, 1981.

Katz, Shmuel, *Days of Fire*, London: W.H. Allen, 1968.

Khalidi, Walid, *Conflict and Violence in Lebanon*, Cambridge: Harvard University Center for International Affairs, 1979.

Magid, Shaul, *The Necessity of Exile*, Brooklyn, N.Y.: Ayin Press, 2023.

Meyer, Lawrence, *Israel Now: Portrait of a Troubled Land*, N. Y.: Delacorte Press, 1982.

Mroz, John Edwin, *Beyond Security—Private Perceptions Among Arabs and Israelis*, N.Y.: International Peace Academy, 1980.

Palgi, Arieh, *Shalom V'Lo Yoteir* (Peace and No More), Tel Aviv, Sifriat Hapoalim, 1979.

Parkin, Frank, *Middle Class Radicalism*, Manchester: Manchester University Press, 1968.

Peace Now pamphlets, Dates: Spring 1978, October 1979, June 1980, October 1980, June 1982, July 1982.

Quandt, William B., Fuad Jabbar and Ann Mosely Lesch, *The Politics of Palestinian Nationalism*, Berkeley: University of California Press, 1973.

Rubenstein, Danny, *On the Lord's Side: Gush Emunim*, (Hebrew), Hakibbutz Hameuchad Publishing House, Ltd., 1982.

Safran, Nadav, *Israel, The Embattled*, Cambridge: Harvard University Press, 1981.

Schectman, Joseph B., and Yehuda Benari, The History of the Revisionist Movement, Tel Aviv: Hadar Publishing Co., 1970.

Smith, Gary V., ed., *Zionism: The Dream and the Reality*, N.Y.: Harper and Row Publishers, Inc., 1974.

Sobel, Lester A., ed., *Peace-Making in the Middle East*, N.Y.: Facts on File, Inc., 1980.

Stone, Russell A., *Social Change In Israel: Attitudes and Events*, 1967-1979, N.Y.: Praeger Publishers, 1982.

Sykes, Christopher, *Crossroads to Israel: 1917-1948*, Bloomington: Indiana University Press, 1965.

Tamarin, Georges R., *The Israeli Dilemma: Essays on a Warfare State*, Rotterdam: Rotterdam University Press, 1973.

Timerman, Jacobo, *The Longest War*, Great Britain: Pan Books, 1982.

Wank, Solomon, ed., *Doves and Diplomats*, Westport, Connecticut: Greenwood Press, 1978.

ARTICLES

Arian, Asher, "Elections 1981: Competitiveness and Polarization," *The Jerusalem Quarterly*, Fall 1981.

Avishai, Bernard, "The Victory of the New Israel," *The New York Review of Books*, August 13, 1981.

Benal, Jolanta, "Peace Maneuvers—An Interview with Me'ir Pa'il," *WIN Magazine*, March 1, 1983.

Bruzonsky, Marc, "Jabotinsky: The Legend and Its Power," *Israel Horizons*, March-April 1981.

Cantarow, Ellen, "Eternal War—Darkness Descends on a Light Unto Nations," *Mother Jones*, December 1982.

Eisenstadt, S.N., "The Oriental Jews in Israel," *Jewish Social Studies*, July 1950.

Elkins, Michael, "Self-Searching in Israel," *The New York Times Magazine*, March 7, 1982.

Fellman, Gordon, "*Israel at a Crossroads—Zionism: Left and Right*," WIN Magazine, January 1, 1983.

BIBLIOGRAPHY

Horowitz, Dan, and Moshe Lissak, "Ideology and Politics in the Yishuv," *The Jerusalem Quarterly*, Winter 1977.

Howard, Esther, "Israel: The Sorcerer's Apprentice," *MERIP Reports*, February, 1983.

Kapeliuk, Amnon, "Eliminating the Palestinian Roadblock—Toward a New Regional Order," translated in Journal of *Palestine Studies*, Summer Fall 1982.

Milson, Menachem, "How to Make Peace with the Palestinians," *Commentary*, May 1981.

Oz, Amos, "Has Israel Altered Its Visions?" *The New York Times Magazine*, July 11, 1982.

Roshwald, M., "Political Parties and Social Classes in Israel," *Social Research*, Summer 1956.

Ryan, Sheila, "Israel's Invasion of Lebanon: Background to the Crisis," *Journal of Palestine Studies*, Summer-Fall 1982.

Shipler, David K., "Israel: Voices of Moral Anguish," *The New York Times Magazine*, February 27, 1983.

Wright, Claudia, "Strategy and Deception in Reagan's Policy Towards the Arabs," *Journal of Palestine Studies*, Spring 1982.

APPENDIX: PEACE AND HUMAN RIGHTS ORGANIZATIONS

B'tselem, The Israeli Information Center for Human Rights in the Occupied Territories: www.btselem.org

Breaking the Silence: www.breakingthesilence.org.il

Combatants for Peace: www.cfpeace.org

Gisha, Legal Center for Freedom of Movement: www.gisha.org

Givat Haviva — The Center for a Shared Society: www.givathaviva.org

Molad, The Center for the Renewal of Israeli Democracy: www.molad.org

Neve Shalom/Wahat as-Salam: www.wasns.org

New Israel Fund: www.nif.org

New Jewish Narrative: www.newjewishnarrative.org

Parents Circle—Families Forum: www.theparentscircle.org

APPENDIX: PEACE AND HUMAN RIGHTS ORGANIZATIONS

Peace Now: www.peacenow.org.il/eng

Physicians for Human Rights: www.phr.org.il/en

Rabbis for Human Rights: www.rhr.org.il/eng

Standing Together: www.standing-together.org/en

Truah—The Rabbinic Call for Human Rights: www.truah.org

Women in Black: www.womeninblack.org

Women Wage Peace: www.womenwagepeace.org.il

Yesh Din: www.yesh-din.org

Yesh Gvul: www.yesh-gvul.org

ABOUT THE AUTHOR

Micah L. Sifry is a writer and editor who has covered many topics including the Middle East, American politics, civic technology, and movement organizing. He is a former associate editor of *The Nation* magazine and the former president and co-founder of Civic Hall, New York City's collaborative community center for civic tech. He currently writes a weekly Substack newsletter on politics, technology, movements and organizing called *The Connector*.

He is a graduate of Princeton University (BA Politics, 1983) and New York University (MA Politics, 1989).

For more information on his work, see MicahSifry.com.

ALSO BY MICAH L. SIFRY

The Gulf War Reader: History, Documents, Opinions, Christopher Cerf, co-editor (Times Books, 1991)

The Iraq War Reader: History, Documents, Opinions, Christopher Cerf, co-editor (Random House, 2002)

Spoiling for a Fight: Third-Party Politics in America (Routledge, 2003)

Is That a Politician in Your Pocket? Nancy Watzman, co-author (Wiley, 2004)

Rebooting America: Ideas for Redesigning American Democracy for the Internet Age, Allison Fine, co-editor (Personal Democracy Press, 2008)

WikiLeaks and the Age of Transparency (OR Books, 2011)

The Big Disconnect: Why the Internet Hasn't Changed Politics (Yet) (OR Books, 2014)

A Lever and a Place to Stand: How Civic Tech Can Move the World, Jessica McKenzie, co-editor (Personal Democracy Press, 2015)

Civic Tech in the Global South, Tiago Peixoto, co-editor (World Bank Books, 2016).

www.ingramcontent.com/pod-product-compliance
Lightning Source LLC
Chambersburg PA
CBHW071250130626
46556CB00003B/1244